- The content of all the major specifications has been distilled to the ess[...] provide you with a set of user-friendly and well organised revision n[...]

- All you need for the exam is here, but don't just read! LEARN ACTIVELY:

- Constantly test yourself, without looking at the book.

- When you have revised a section or a diagram, PLACE A TICK AGAINST IT. Similarly, tick the "Progress and Revision" section of the contents when you have done a page. This is great for your self-confidence.

- Many questions depend only on straightforward recall of facts, so make sure you learn them!

This guide has been checked against the exam board specifications for examination in 2007 onwards. The content has been revised and updated where necessary to ensure that it is as relevant and accurate as ever.

IMPORTANT POINT: Energy is often referred to as being "used". In this guide for greater scientific accuracy we refer to it being "transferred" into other forms.

CONSULTANT EDITORS ...
DON WEBSTER
CLARE TOWNSEND
DAVID CHARLES

Many thanks to the HUDDERSFIELD EXAMINER for allowing us to reproduce action photographs from their archives and in particular to Lynda Thwaites for helping us to select them.

- Thanks also to Barry Adams for taking the pupil photographs

© 2002 LONSDALE. ALL RIGHTS RESERVED. NO PART OF THIS PUBLICATION MAY BE REPRODUCED, STORED IN A RETRIEVAL SYSTEM, OR TRANSMITTED IN ANY FORM OR BY ANY MEANS, ELECTRONIC, MECHANICAL, PHOTOCOPYING, RECORDING, OR OTHERWISE WITHOUT THE PRIOR WRITTEN PERMISSION OF LONSDALE.

Lonsdale School Revision Guides

CONTENTS

Covered in Class | Revised | Revised | Page No.

The Human Body

Page	Topic
4	Health And Fitness
5	The Skeleton
6	The Vertebral Column
7	Types Of Joint
8	Movements Of Joints
9	Muscles
10	How Muscles Work
11	The Components Of The Circulatory System
12	The Blood Vessels And Blood
13	Monitoring The Circulation
14	The Breathing System
15	Breathing And Capacity For Gas Exchange
16	Energy From Food
17	Respiration 1 - Aerobic
18	Respiration 2 - Anaerobic
19	The Nervous And Hormonal Systems
20	Energy Requirements
21	Diet And Nutrition
22	Special Diets

Training And Exercise

23	Reasons For Exercise
24	The Principles Of Training
25	Muscular Endurance And Strength
26	Muscular Strength
27	Speed
28	Flexibility 1
29	Flexibility 2
30	Aerobic And Anaerobic Training
31	Specific Training Methods 1
32	Specific Training Methods 2
33	Specific Training Methods 3
34	Training Requirements For Sport
35	Long Term Effects Of Training
36	The Body's Response To Exercise
37	Temperature Regulation And Water Balance
38	Fitness Testing
39	Testing Specific Fitness

Aspects Of Sport

Page	Topic
40	Prevention Of Injury
41	Footwear For Sport
42	Playing Safe
43	Personal Hygiene
44	Posture

Lonsdale School Revision Guides

CONTENTS

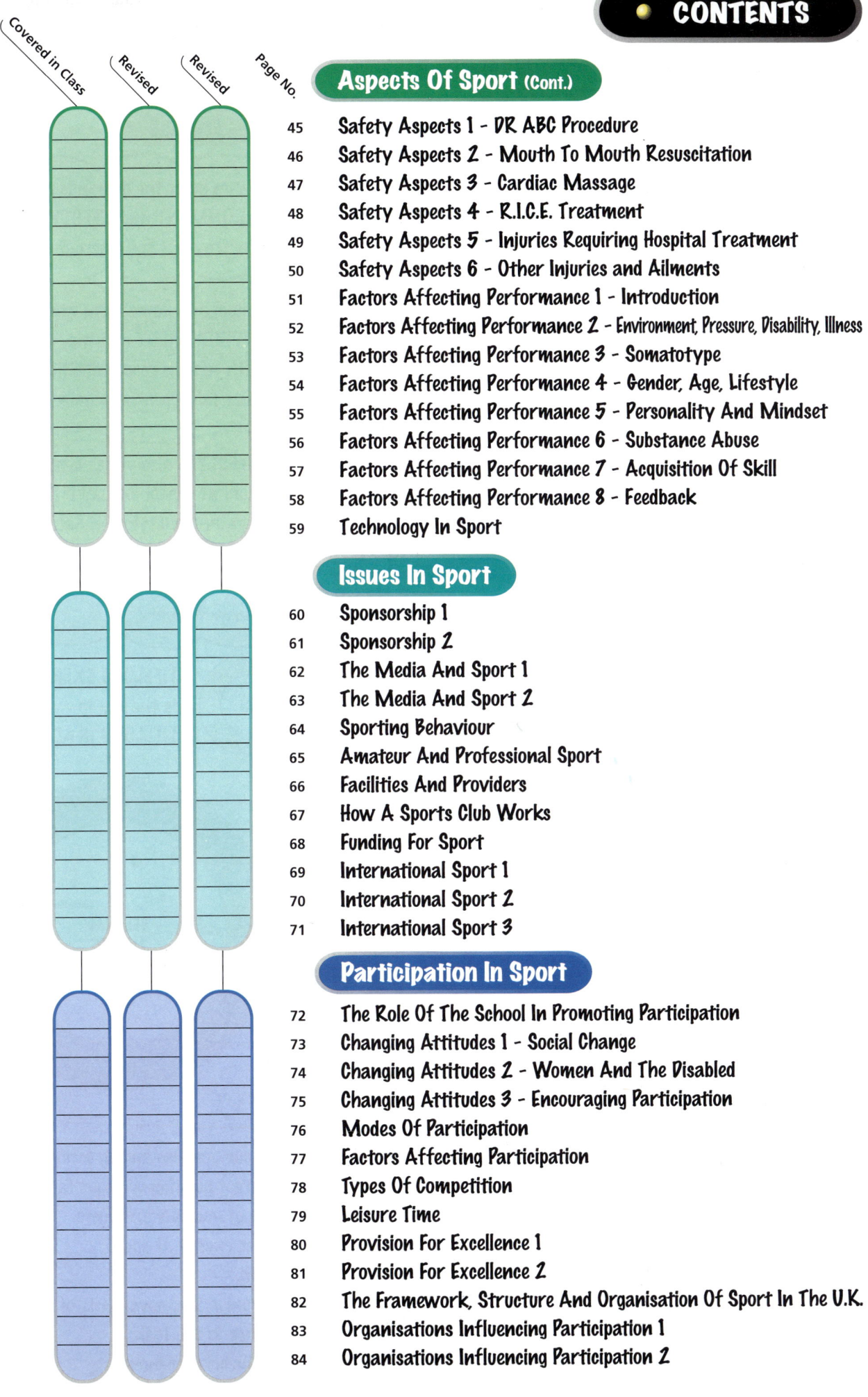

Aspects Of Sport (Cont.)

Page No.	
45	Safety Aspects 1 - DR ABC Procedure
46	Safety Aspects 2 - Mouth To Mouth Resuscitation
47	Safety Aspects 3 - Cardiac Massage
48	Safety Aspects 4 - R.I.C.E. Treatment
49	Safety Aspects 5 - Injuries Requiring Hospital Treatment
50	Safety Aspects 6 - Other Injuries and Ailments
51	Factors Affecting Performance 1 - Introduction
52	Factors Affecting Performance 2 - Environment, Pressure, Disability, Illness
53	Factors Affecting Performance 3 - Somatotype
54	Factors Affecting Performance 4 - Gender, Age, Lifestyle
55	Factors Affecting Performance 5 - Personality And Mindset
56	Factors Affecting Performance 6 - Substance Abuse
57	Factors Affecting Performance 7 - Acquisition Of Skill
58	Factors Affecting Performance 8 - Feedback
59	Technology In Sport

Issues In Sport

60	Sponsorship 1
61	Sponsorship 2
62	The Media And Sport 1
63	The Media And Sport 2
64	Sporting Behaviour
65	Amateur And Professional Sport
66	Facilities And Providers
67	How A Sports Club Works
68	Funding For Sport
69	International Sport 1
70	International Sport 2
71	International Sport 3

Participation In Sport

72	The Role Of The School In Promoting Participation
73	Changing Attitudes 1 - Social Change
74	Changing Attitudes 2 - Women And The Disabled
75	Changing Attitudes 3 - Encouraging Participation
76	Modes Of Participation
77	Factors Affecting Participation
78	Types Of Competition
79	Leisure Time
80	Provision For Excellence 1
81	Provision For Excellence 2
82	The Framework, Structure And Organisation Of Sport In The U.K.
83	Organisations Influencing Participation 1
84	Organisations Influencing Participation 2
85	Index

HEALTH AND FITNESS

The Human Body — 1

Definitions Of Health And Fitness

HEALTH

'A state of complete PHYSICAL, MENTAL and SOCIAL WELL BEING'.

- PHYSICALLY, all my body systems are working well, and I have no illness or injuries.
- MENTALLY, I feel good about myself, my emotions are under control and I don't feel stressed.
- SOCIALLY, I have all the basic necessities of life, the support of friends, and an awareness of my role in society.

FITNESS

'The ability to meet the demands of your ENVIRONMENT and LIFESTYLE' and still have energy left for emergencies

- School and home form my immediate ENVIRONMENT and they present me with certain responsibilities which I must face up to on a daily basis.
- My LIFESTYLE also places demands on me e.g. sport at school, my part-time job on Sundays, and partying on Saturday night!
- Because I'm reasonably fit, I cope with my life with energy to spare.

PHYSICAL EXERCISE is the key which links HEALTH and FITNESS.

HEALTH — PHYSICAL EXERCISE — FITNESS

LIFELONG EXERCISE is the key to LIFELONG HEALTH.

Physical Fitness And Motor Fitness

1. GENERAL FITNESS

- This is sometimes called health-related fitness because it relates to the type of fitness required by a normal person to cope with the daily demands made of them.
- The five components vary in their necessity from person to person. Fitness is relative and is specific to your own environment. A person working at a desk in an office would not necessarily need to be as physically fit as someone labouring on a building site. They may need to be mentally more fit, however.

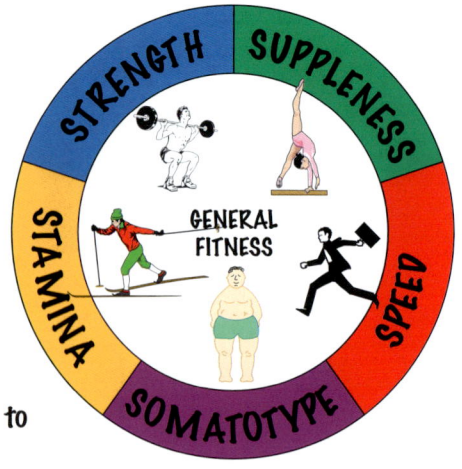

GENERAL FITNESS: STRENGTH, SUPPLENESS, SPEED, SOMATOTYPE, STAMINA

2. MOTOR FITNESS

AGILITY — being able to alter your position and direction at speed.

BALANCE — maintaining the correct position without faltering during the execution of your performance.

POWER — being able to transfer energy at speed i.e. explosive strength.

COORDINATION — being able to synchronise the movements of different body parts in response to the task.

TIMING — acting at precisely the correct moment.

REACTION TIME — the time it takes to react i.e. your speed of thought and action.

THE SKELETON

The Human Body — 2

The Skeleton

The skeleton gives the body its shape. It is made up of 206 bones in total, which come in FOUR types, LONG BONES, SHORT BONES, FLAT BONES and IRREGULAR BONES. These are held together by joints.

PROTECTION

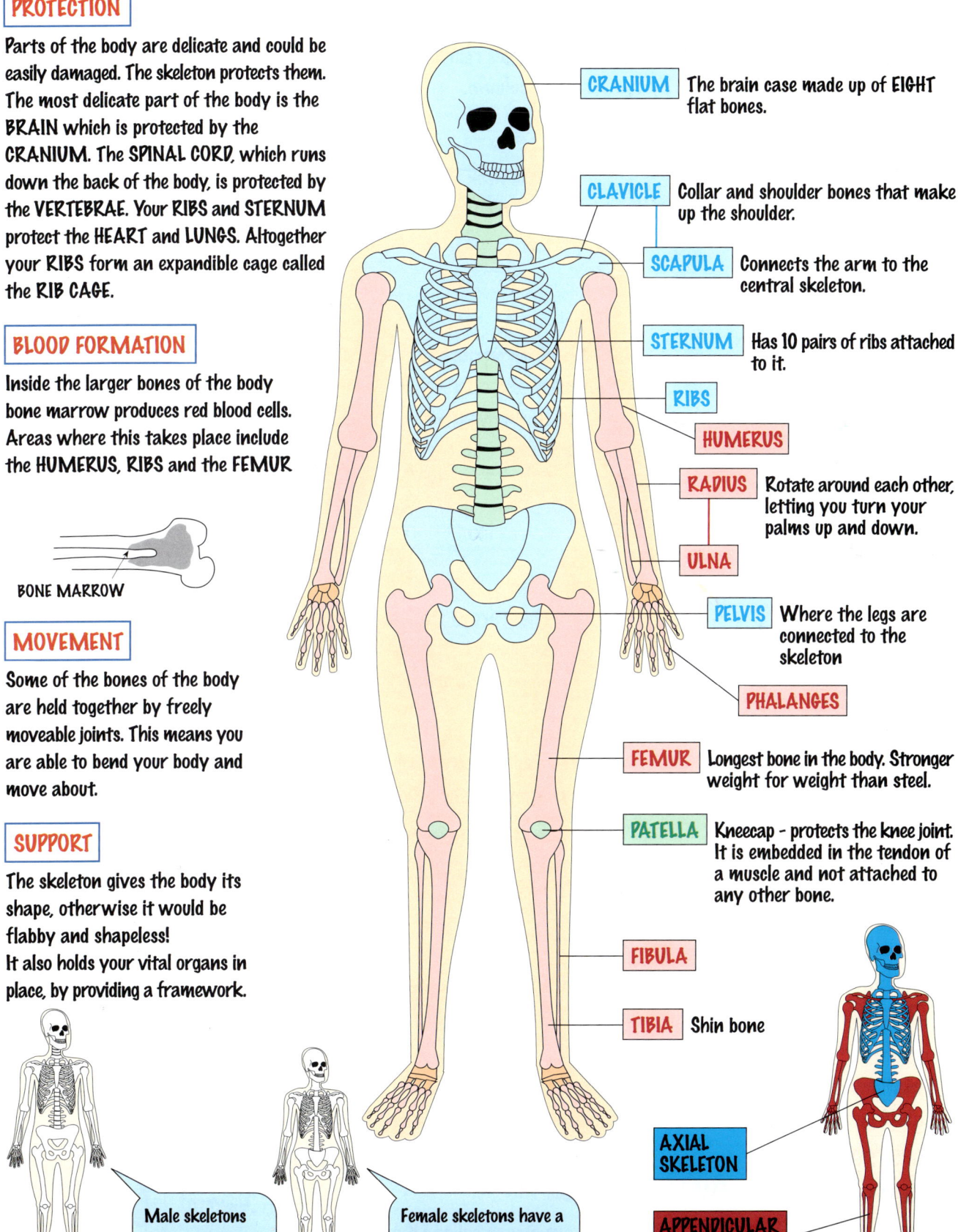

Parts of the body are delicate and could be easily damaged. The skeleton protects them. The most delicate part of the body is the BRAIN which is protected by the CRANIUM. The SPINAL CORD, which runs down the back of the body, is protected by the VERTEBRAE. Your RIBS and STERNUM protect the HEART and LUNGS. Altogether your RIBS form an expandible cage called the RIB CAGE.

BLOOD FORMATION

Inside the larger bones of the body bone marrow produces red blood cells. Areas where this takes place include the HUMERUS, RIBS and the FEMUR

BONE MARROW

MOVEMENT

Some of the bones of the body are held together by freely moveable joints. This means you are able to bend your body and move about.

SUPPORT

The skeleton gives the body its shape, otherwise it would be flabby and shapeless!
It also holds your vital organs in place, by providing a framework.

CRANIUM — The brain case made up of EIGHT flat bones.

CLAVICLE — Collar and shoulder bones that make up the shoulder.

SCAPULA — Connects the arm to the central skeleton.

STERNUM — Has 10 pairs of ribs attached to it.

RIBS

HUMERUS

RADIUS — Rotate around each other, letting you turn your palms up and down.

ULNA

PELVIS — Where the legs are connected to the skeleton

PHALANGES

FEMUR — Longest bone in the body. Stronger weight for weight than steel.

PATELLA — Kneecap - protects the knee joint. It is embedded in the tendon of a muscle and not attached to any other bone.

FIBULA

TIBIA — Shin bone

Male skeletons tend to be bigger.

Female skeletons have a wider pelvis so that it is easier to have children.

AXIAL SKELETON

APPENDICULAR SKELETON

THE VERTEBRAL COLUMN

The Human Body — 3

The Vertebral Column

The vertebral column has 3 main functions ...
- ... **SUPPORT.** It is literally the "backbone" of the body and as such transfers the weight of the body downwards to the pelvis.
- ... **MOVEMENT.** Even though the individual vertebrae are held together by slightly moveable joints, the presence of so many of them allows great flexibility.
- ... **PROTECTION.** The spinal cord, a bundle of nerves relaying information to and from the brain, runs through and is protected by the vertebral column.

7 CERVICAL VERTEBRAE — These neck vertebrae allow your head to bend, tilt and nod. The first two (atlas and axis) allow rotation of the head.

12 THORACIC VERTEBRAE — These vertebrae have projections for attachment of the ribs. Flexion and extension can occur and a small degree of rotation, but this movement is limited compared to the cervical vertebrae.

5 LUMBAR VERTEBRAE — These are in the waist region and have to endure the greatest amount of stress in walking and support. Therefore they are large and provide attachment for the back muscles.

5 SACRAL VERTEBRAE — These five vertebrae are fused to form one piece, and together with the pelvis form the pelvic (hip) girdle to which the legs are attached.

4 COCCYX — These form the remnants of what was once a tail in our evolutionary past. These are also fused together.

Joining Bones To Bones

- Where two bones meet, the surfaces rub against one another as movement occurs. To reduce the amount of friction, a layer of SMOOTH CARTILAGE covers the ends.
- In the vertebral column, the cartilage forms discs which act as shock absorbers between each individual vertebrae.
- In SYNOVIAL JOINTS, friction is also reduced by a thin layer of lubricating liquid called SYNOVIAL FLUID (see next page).
- Holding the bones together are tough, fibrous straps called LIGAMENTS. These are reasonably elastic to allow movement at the joint.

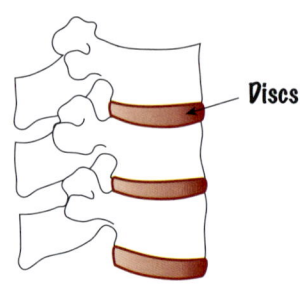

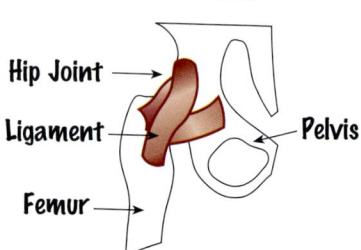

TYPES OF JOINT

The Human Body — 4

Immovable (Fixed) Joints

- These occur where movement would be a severe disadvantage e.g. the bones of the cranium, the joint between the pelvis and the vertebral column.
- The joints are held together by tough, fibrous tissue which develops during childhood.

Slightly Moveable Joints

- Here, movement is needed but only to a certain point e.g. the vertebral column.
- Individual vertebrae are separated by cartilage and held together by tough, fibrous bands called ligaments (see previous page).

Freely Moveable Joints

These are also called SYNOVIAL joints, and occur in most places in the body where a reasonable degree of movement occurs.

- Characteristically they are surrounded by a CAPSULE, the internal lining of which secretes SYNOVIAL FLUID to LUBRICATE the joint.

- TOUGH OUTER LIGAMENTS
- CAPSULE OF THE JOINT
- SYNOVIAL MEMBRANE
- SYNOVIAL FLUID
- CARTILAGE

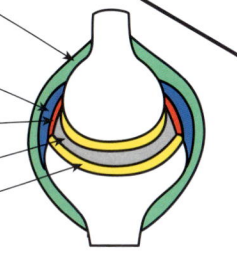

A Synovial Joint

Types Of Freely Moveable Joint

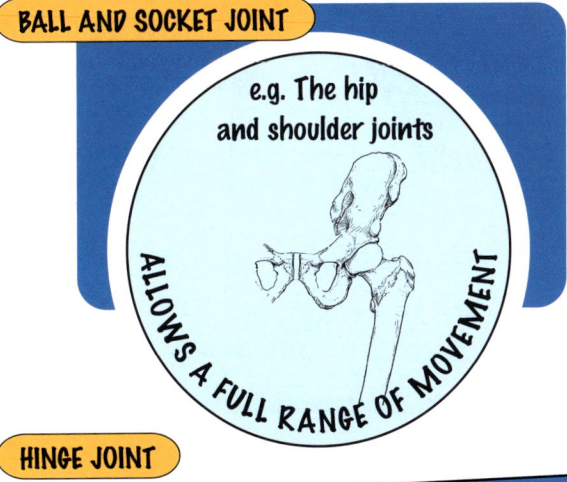

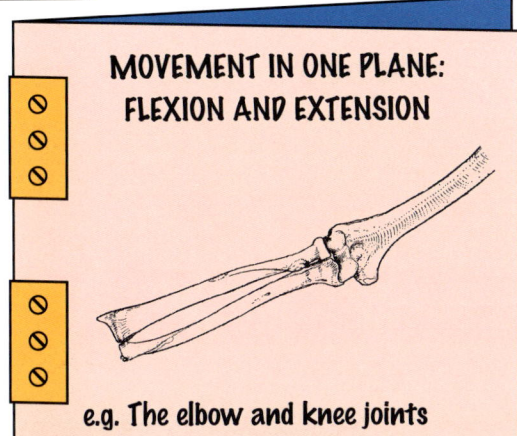

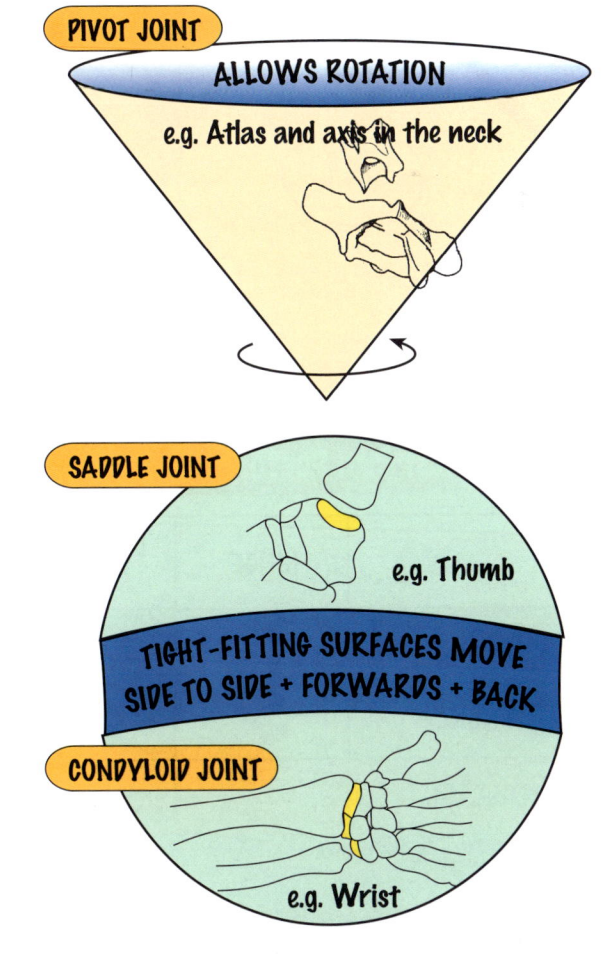

BALL AND SOCKET JOINT
e.g. The hip and shoulder joints
ALLOWS A FULL RANGE OF MOVEMENT

PIVOT JOINT
ALLOWS ROTATION
e.g. Atlas and axis in the neck

HINGE JOINT
MOVEMENT IN ONE PLANE: FLEXION AND EXTENSION
e.g. The elbow and knee joints

SADDLE JOINT
e.g. Thumb
TIGHT-FITTING SURFACES MOVE SIDE TO SIDE + FORWARDS + BACK

CONDYLOID JOINT
e.g. Wrist

GLIDING JOINTS

These occur in the many small bones of the hands and feet. They allow a slight sliding motion forwards and backwards and from side to side.

Lonsdale School Revision Guides

MOVEMENTS OF JOINTS

The Human Body — 5

Types Of Movement In Relation To Physical Activities

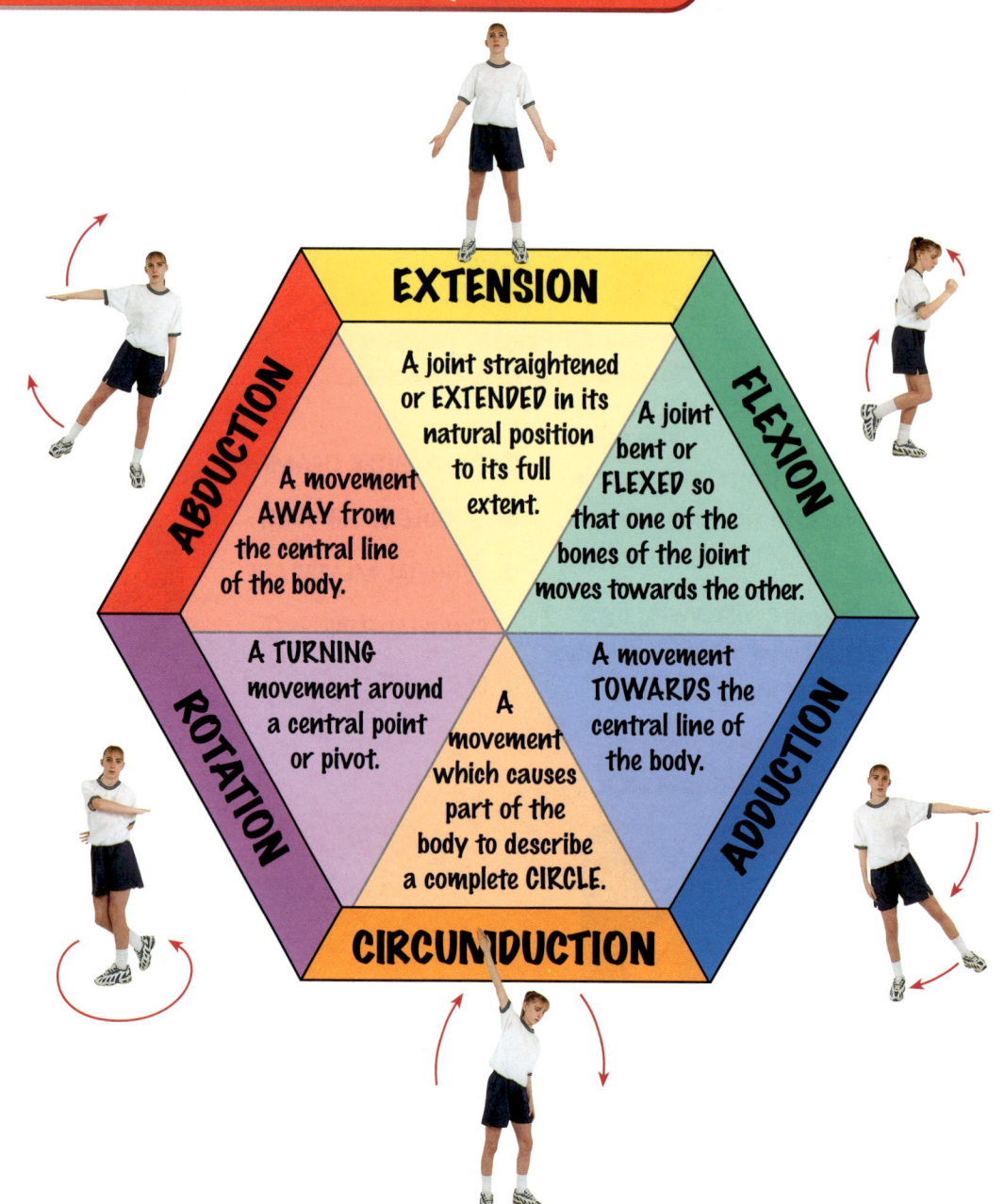

EXTENSION — A joint straightened or EXTENDED in its natural position to its full extent.

FLEXION — A joint bent or FLEXED so that one of the bones of the joint moves towards the other.

ABDUCTION — A movement AWAY from the central line of the body.

ADDUCTION — A movement TOWARDS the central line of the body.

ROTATION — A TURNING movement around a central point or pivot.

CIRCUMDUCTION — A movement which causes part of the body to describe a complete CIRCLE.

Joints That Can Perform These Movements

	HINGE	BALL AND SOCKET	PIVOT	CONDYLOID	SADDLE	GLIDING
FLEXION	✓	✓		✓	✓	A SMALL AMOUNT OF THESE TYPES OF MOVEMENT
EXTENSION	✓	✓		✓	✓	
ABDUCTION		✓		✓	✓	
ADDUCTION		✓		✓	✓	
ROTATION		✓	✓			
CIRCUMDUCTION		✓				

Lonsdale School Revision Guides

MUSCLES

The Human Body — 6

Every movement of your body depends on muscles. These are three different types of muscle.

1. INVOLUNTARY (Smooth)
- Found mainly surrounding hollow organs e.g. blood vessels, gut.
- Performs its function without any conscious control, but usually quite slowly.

2. VOLUNTARY (Skeletal)
- Found mainly attached to the skeleton.
- Capable of rapid contraction which causes skeletal movement.
- Under conscious control e.g. all conscious movement.

3. CARDIAC
- Found only in the walls of the heart.
- Undergoes constant automatic rhythmical contractions.
- No conscious control.

Voluntary Muscles – How They Perform In Detail

FRONT

PECTORALS — Create adduction at the shoulder across the chest, e.g. press-ups.

ABDOMINALS — Allow you to flex your trunk, e.g. sit-ups.

QUADRICEPS — Makes extension of the leg possible at the knee, e.g. squats, kicking.

DELTOIDS — Create abduction at the shoulder and raise your arm sideways, e.g. swimming arm action.

BICEPS — Allows flexion at the elbow, e.g. chin-ups.

BACK

TRAPEZIUS — Allows rotation of the shoulders, e.g. cricket bowling action.

TRICEPS — Creates extension at the elbow. e.g. press-ups, throwing.

GASTROCNEMIUS — Allows you to stand on your tiptoes, by creating extension at the ankle, e.g. sprinting (start).

LATISSIMUS — Adduction at the shoulder behind your back, e.g. rope climb.

GLUTEALS — Allow extension, abduction and adduction at the hip. (Gluteus Maximus is the biggest Gluteal). e.g. squats, jumping.

HAMSTRINGS — These allow flexion of the leg at the knee, e.g. sprinting (leg action recovery).

Muscle Attachment

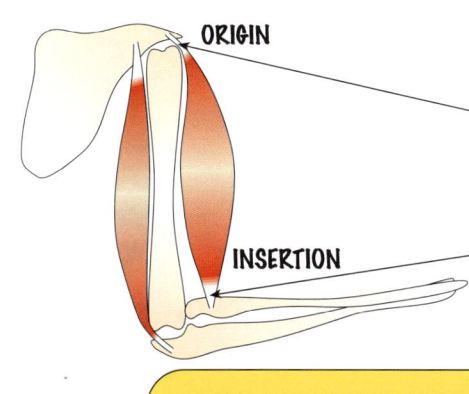

ORIGIN

INSERTION

Voluntary muscles are attached to your skeleton by **TENDONS**, usually across a synovial joint. These are fibrous and INELASTIC.

A The point where the muscle tendon attaches to the fixed or stationary bone is called the **ORIGIN**.

B The point where the muscle tendon attaches to the moving bone is called the **INSERTION**.

As muscles contract they shorten. This makes the joint move.

WHEN A MUSCLE CONTRACTS THE INSERTION MOVES TOWARDS THE ORIGIN.

Lonsdale School Revision Guides

HOW MUSCLES WORK

The Human Body — 7

Muscles can only create movement in ONE direction ... by becoming SHORTER!!

> This means you need TWO muscles at every joint to allow movement in TWO directions.

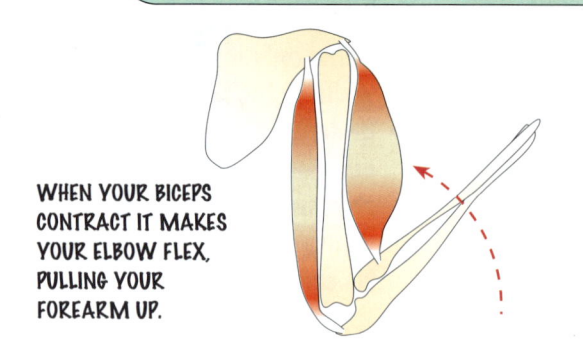

SO MUSCLES WORK IN PAIRS.

WHEN YOUR BICEPS CONTRACT IT MAKES YOUR ELBOW FLEX, PULLING YOUR FOREARM UP.

TO ALLOW YOUR ELBOW TO EXTEND, YOU NEED YOUR TRICEPS TO CONTRACT AND PULL YOUR ARM BACK DOWN. (OR RELY ON GRAVITY!)

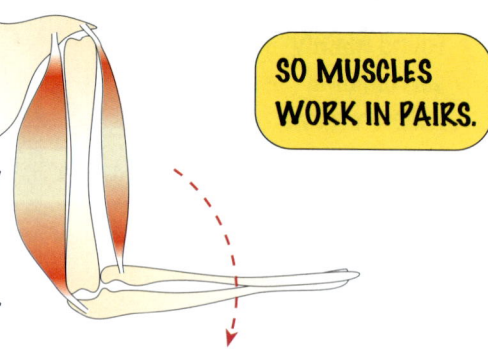

Muscles working in opposite directions like this are said to be working ANTAGONISTICALLY. The muscle doing the work and creating the movement is called the AGONIST or PRIME MOVER. The muscle which is relaxing and letting the movement take place, is called the ANTAGONIST.

So, in the example of the arm, when you flex your elbow, e.g. during a bicep curl the bicep is the AGONIST and the tricep is the ANTAGONIST.

When other muscles ASSIST the PRIME MOVER in creating a movement, these other muscles are called SYNERGISTS. e.g. deltoids doing press-ups

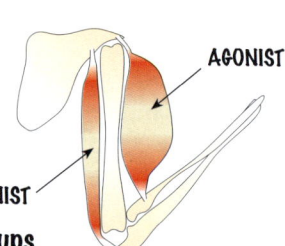

Types Of Muscle Contraction

1. ISOMETRIC CONTRACTION
- Here, the muscle stays the SAME LENGTH as it works and so no movement occurs.
- The muscles in the vertebral column contract isometrically to maintain our posture.

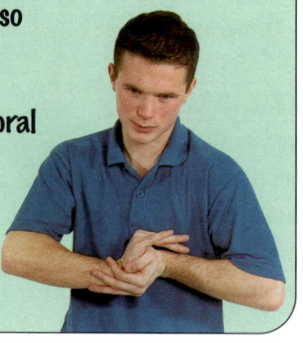

2. ISOTONIC CONTRACTION
- Here, the muscle CHANGES ITS LENGTH as it works ...
- Shortening is called CONCENTRIC CONTRACTION, and lengthening under tension is called ECCENTRIC CONTRACTION.

All muscles have fast and slow twitch fibres or a mixture of the two. The proportions are inherited.

FAST TWITCH FIBRES
- Produce POWERFUL contractions VERY QUICKLY (EXPLOSIVE).
- These fibres become FATIGUED in a short time.
- Great for sprinting and fast bowling.

SLOW TWITCH FIBRES
- Produce slower contractions.
- Become fatigued less quickly.
- Ideal for endurance events. e.g. marathon running.

THE COMPONENTS OF THE CIRCULATORY SYSTEM — The Human Body — 8

The Function Of The Circulatory System

The circulatory system has three main parts – the heart, the blood and the blood vessels – and is connected to the lungs. Its function is to pump blood around the body. The blood...

- transports oxygen, carbon dioxide, nutrients and waste products
- helps to control body temperature
- repairs damaged body tissue, e.g. bruising and clotting at open wounds
- fights disease and harmful bacteria that enter the body.

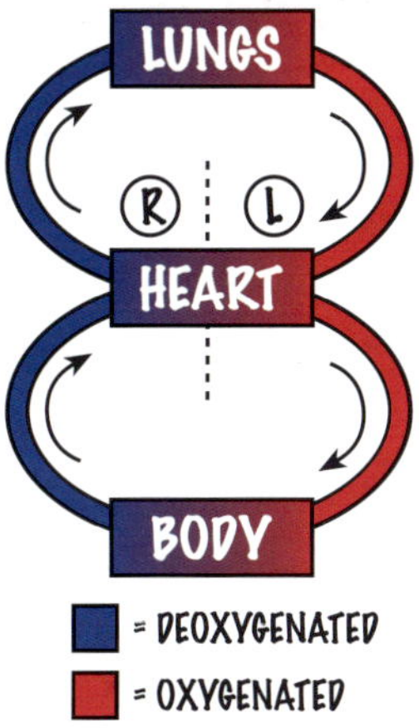

■ = DEOXYGENATED
■ = OXYGENATED

The Heart And Major Blood Vessels

The heart acts as a PUMP in a DOUBLE CIRCULATORY SYSTEM.

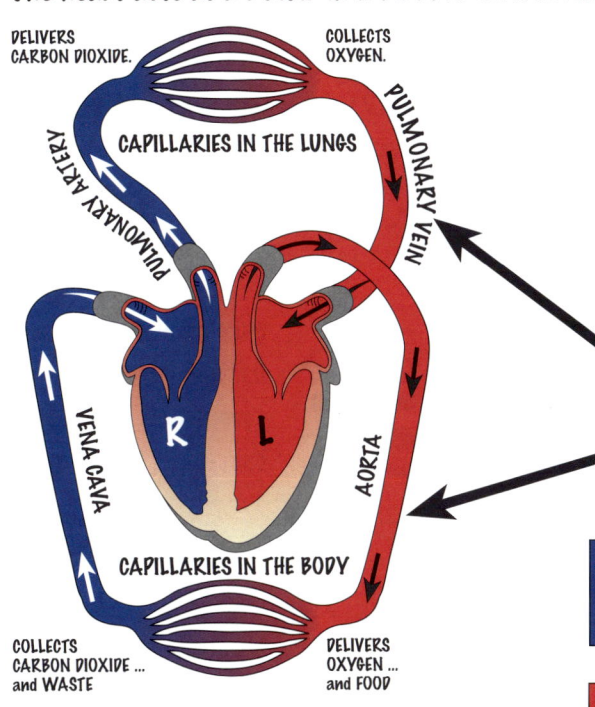

DELIVERS CARBON DIOXIDE.
COLLECTS OXYGEN.
CAPILLARIES IN THE LUNGS
PULMONARY ARTERY
PULMONARY VEIN
VENA CAVA
AORTA
CAPILLARIES IN THE BODY
COLLECTS CARBON DIOXIDE ... and WASTE
DELIVERS OXYGEN ... and FOOD

■ Blood low in oxygen (DEOXYGENATED)
■ Blood rich in oxygen (OXYGENATED)

- As you can see blood flows around a 'figure of eight' circuit and passes through the heart TWICE on each circuit.
- Blood travels AWAY from the heart through ARTERIES, ...
- ... and returns to the heart through VEINS.

There are TWO SEPARATE CIRCULATION SYSTEMS, ...

One 'loop' carries blood from the HEART to the LUNGS and then back to the HEART ...

... and the other carries blood from the HEART to ALL OTHER PARTS OF THE BODY and then back to the HEART.

The RIGHT SIDE of the heart pumps blood which is LOW IN OXYGEN to the LUNGS, to pick up OXYGEN.

The LEFT SIDE of the heart pumps blood which is RICH IN OXYGEN to all other parts of the BODY.

How The Heart Pumps Blood

For substances to be delivered and removed from the cells efficiently, the blood must flow at an appropriate rate. The regular contracting and relaxing of the heart ensures this ...

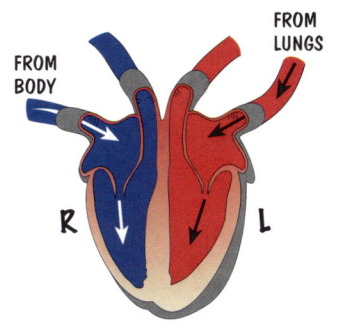

FROM BODY
FROM LUNGS

TO LUNGS
TO BODY

- During RELAXATION PHASE, blood flows into the heart from the lungs and body.
- The upper chambers then squeeze blood into the lower chambers.

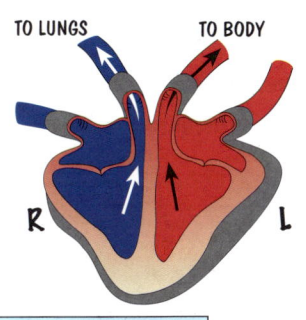

- During CONTRACTION PHASE, the lower chambers contract forcing blood to the body and lungs.
- The cycle then starts again.

THE BLOOD VESSELS AND BLOOD

The Human Body — 9

The Three Types Of Blood Vessel

ARTERY
- Thick, elastic wall to cope with high pressure ...
- ... of blood expelled from the heart.
- Rich in OXYGEN and FOOD.

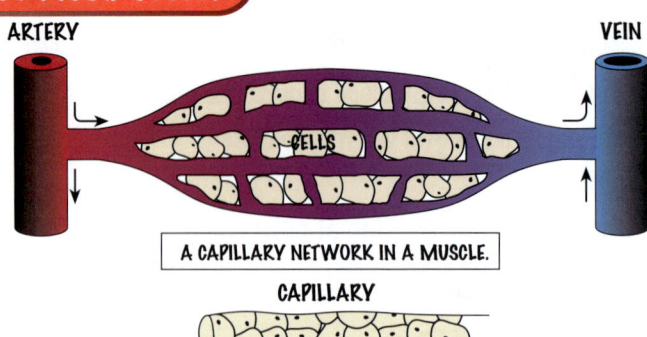

A CAPILLARY NETWORK IN A MUSCLE.

CAPILLARY
- Narrow, thin-walled vessels ...
- ... just one cell thick.

VEIN
- Thinner, less elastic walls ...
- ... containing valves to ...
- ... prevent backflow of blood on the way back to the heart.
- Rich in CARBON DIOXIDE and WASTE.

Exchange Of Substances At The Capillaries

The heart and blood vessels provide a route around the body, but it is the BLOOD which actually TRANSPORTS substances. Exchange of substances between the blood and the body tissues can ONLY OCCUR IN CAPILLARIES. Substances diffuse from the blood into the cells and vice versa. The cells exchange carbon dioxide and waste for oxygen and food.

- Food (e.g. glucose) from the digestive system or the liver is carried in the plasma.
- Oxygen from the lungs is carried by the Red Blood Cells.

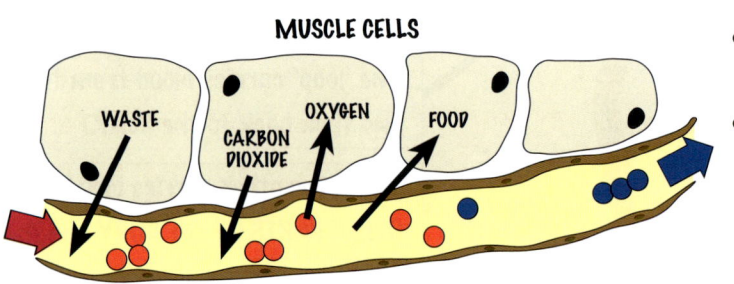

A CAPILLARY VESSEL (one cell thick)

- Waste from the cells is carried in the plasma.
- Carbon dioxide from respiration in the cells is carried in the plasma.

The Blood

If blood is allowed to stand without clotting, it separates out into its 4 components ...

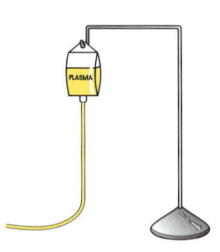

PLASMA is a straw-coloured liquid which transports
- ... Carbon dioxide from the cells to the lungs ...
- ... Glucose from the small intestine to the cells ...
- ... wastes (e.g. Urea) from the cells.

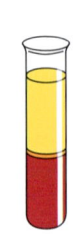

WHITE CELLS have a nucleus which is variable in shape.
- Some engulf invading microbes to defend the body ...
- ... while others produce ANTIBODIES to attack them.
- There's 1 white cell for every 600 red cells!!

PLATELETS are tiny pieces of cell which have no nucleus.
- They clump together when a blood vessel is damaged ...
- ... and form a meshwork of fibres to produce a CLOT.

RED CELLS have no nucleus at all ...
- ... so that they can pack in more HAEMOGLOBIN!
- Haemoglobin carries oxygen in the cell.

MONITORING THE CIRCULATION

The Human Body — 10

Blood Pressure

This is measured using a SPHYGMOMANOMETER which consists of an inflatable cuff through which a variable pressure can be applied to the arm. A stethoscope is used to listen for the sounds of blood flow as the cuff is deflated to a pressure low enough to allow blood flow. The first set of sounds to be heard indicate the SYSTOLIC PRESSURE i.e. when the ventricles are contracting. As the cuff pressure falls the sound becomes louder then suddenly becomes muffled and disappears. The point at which the sound becomes muffled indicates DIASTOLIC PRESSURE i.e. during relaxation of the ventricles. Typical blood pressure might be 120/80 mmHg. (the 120mmHg being the systolic pressure; mmHg is the pressure in millimetres of mercury).

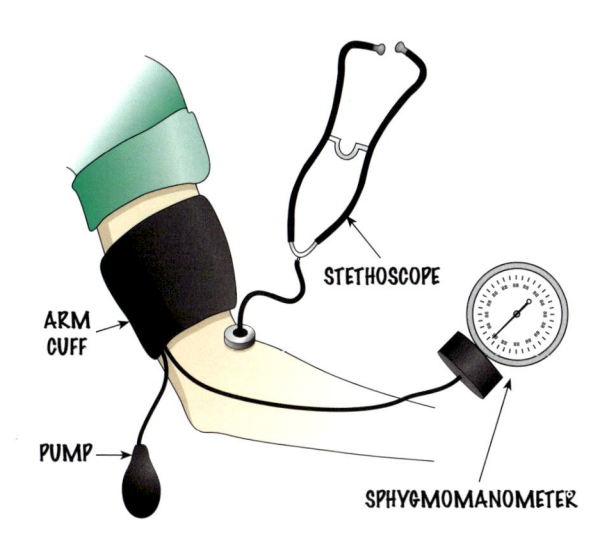

Labels: ARM CUFF, PUMP, STETHOSCOPE, SPHYGMOMANOMETER

Pulse

The arterial pulse is a pressure wave travelling along the thick elastic wall of the arteries, and NOT blood flowing through the arteries. It corresponds with the contraction of the ventricles and can be measured wherever an artery passes close to the surface e.g.

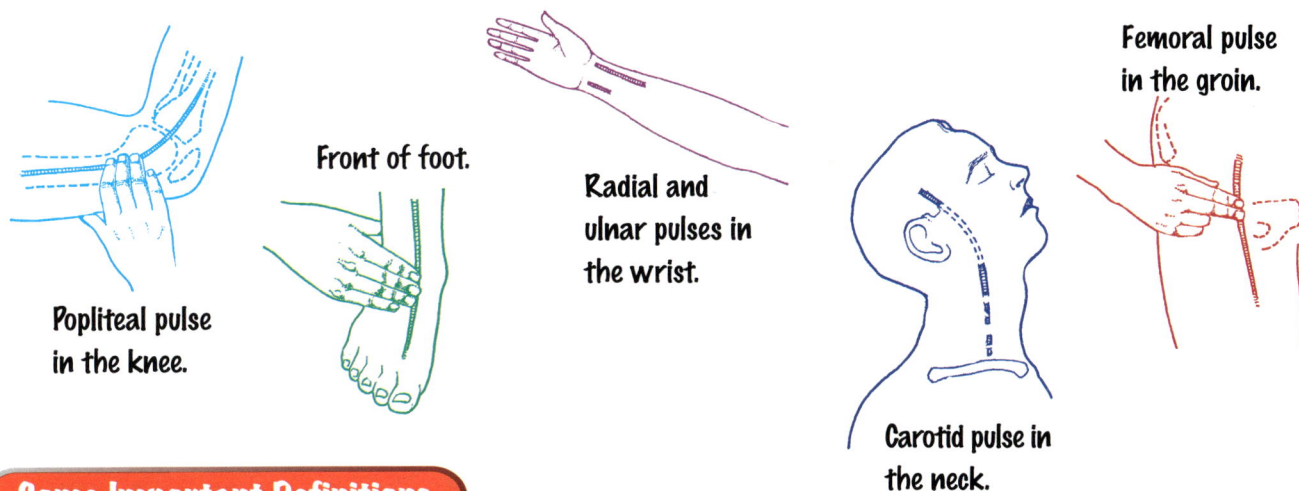

- Popliteal pulse in the knee.
- Front of foot.
- Radial and ulnar pulses in the wrist.
- Carotid pulse in the neck.
- Femoral pulse in the groin.

Some Important Definitions

HEART RATE is the number of 'beats' per minute.
i.e. the number of times the ventricles contract each minute. It is usually measured by taking the pulse.

STROKE VOLUME is the 'output per ventricle PER BEAT'.
i.e. the volume in ml. or cm^3 pumped out by the ventricles each time they contract.

CARDIAC OUTPUT is the 'output per ventricle PER MINUTE'.
i.e. the volume in ml. or cm^3 pumped out by the ventricles every minute.

CARDIAC OUTPUT = STROKE VOLUME × HEART RATE

As exercise intensity increases, HEART RATE increases. Many athletes MONITOR HEART RATE to establish the appropriate level of TRAINING INTENSITY.

THE BREATHING SYSTEM

The Human Body — 11

The Standard Respiratory System Diagram

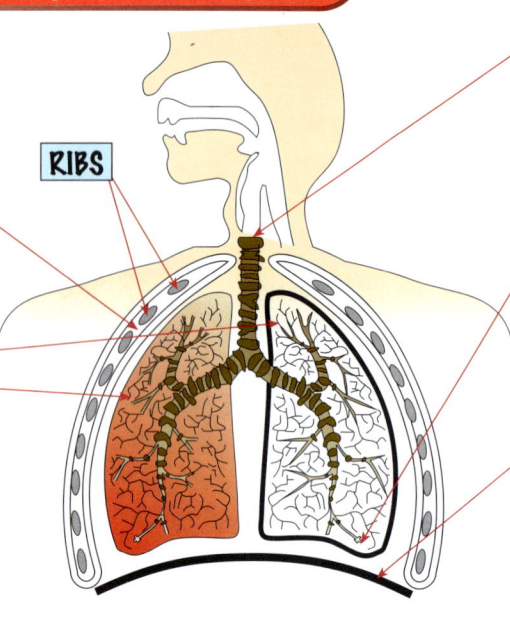

INTERCOSTAL MUSCLES
These raise and lower the ribs during breathing.

RIBS

LUNGS
These are two elastic sacs which have very thin walls. They consist of millions of alveoli.

TRACHEA (windpipe)
This is a large flexible tube surrounded by rings of cartilage to prevent it from collapsing.

ALVEOLI
These are millions of tiny air sacs which make up the lung tissue, and allow gas exchange to occur.

DIAPHRAGM
This is a muscular 'sheet' which divides the chest cavity from the abdomen and is an important muscle in breathing.

Gaseous Exchange In The Alveoli

- The bronchi branch into tiny air tubes which end in a cluster of ALVEOLI.
- The alveoli have a massive blood supply in close contact.
- Oxygen and Carbon dioxide are exchanged between the alveoli and the blood.

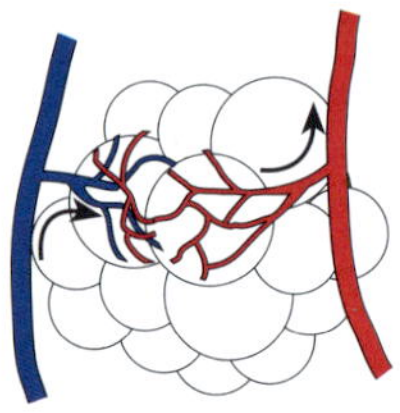

Carbon dioxide leaves the lungs and is breathed out.

Deoxygenated blood rich in carbon dioxide from the body cells arrives at the alveoli.

Carbon dioxide diffuses into the alveoli from the blood plasma.

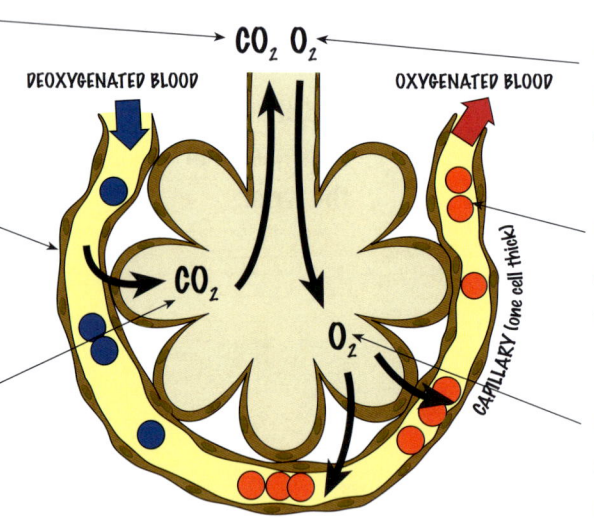

CO_2 O_2

DEOXYGENATED BLOOD   OXYGENATED BLOOD

CAPILLARY (one cell thick)

Oxygen is continually breathed in to replace that picked up by the red cells.

Oxygenated blood leaves the alveoli carrying oxygen to all the cells of the body.

Oxygen diffuses from the alveoli into the blood and is picked up by the red blood cells.

A SINGLE ALVEOLUS AND A CAPILLARY.

A Comparison Of Inhaled Air And Exhaled Air

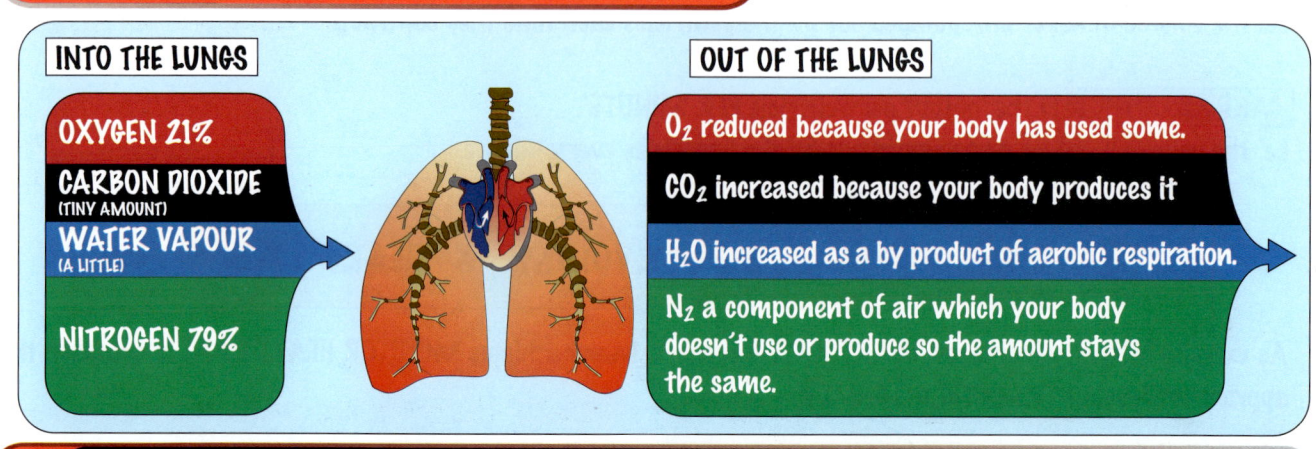

INTO THE LUNGS
- OXYGEN 21%
- CARBON DIOXIDE (TINY AMOUNT)
- WATER VAPOUR (A LITTLE)
- NITROGEN 79%

OUT OF THE LUNGS
- O_2 reduced because your body has used some.
- CO_2 increased because your body produces it
- H_2O increased as a by product of aerobic respiration.
- N_2 a component of air which your body doesn't use or produce so the amount stays the same.

Lonsdale School Revision Guides

BREATHING AND CAPACITY FOR GAS EXCHANGE
The Human Body — 12

Breathing

In breathing we first must make the volume of the thorax (chest) larger, in order to breathe in. Then we make the volume smaller again in order to breathe out ...

It's the same principle with the SYRINGE and the BELLOWS ...

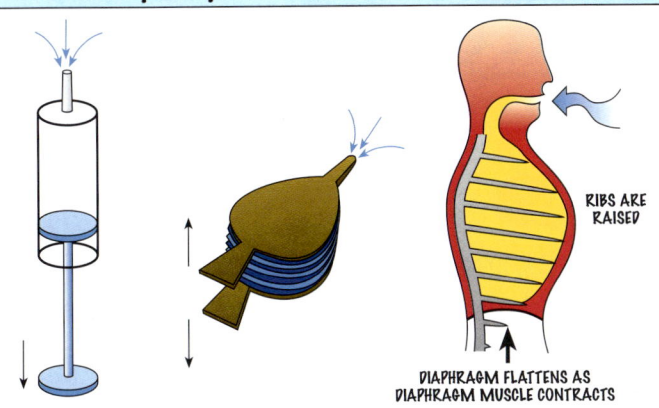

RIBS ARE RAISED

DIAPHRAGM FLATTENS AS DIAPHRAGM MUSCLE CONTRACTS

AN INCREASE IN VOLUME CAUSES A DECREASE IN PRESSURE - and air enters

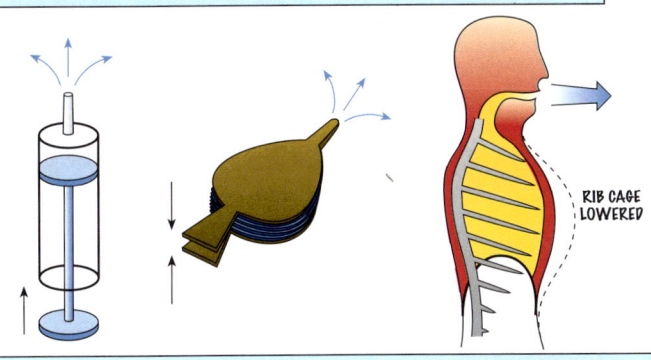

RIB CAGE LOWERED

A DECREASE IN VOLUME CAUSES AN INCREASE IN PRESSURE - and air is forced out.

To inhale:
- The muscles between the ribs contract, pulling the rib cage upwards - a bit like the handle on a bucket.
- At the same time the diaphragm muscles contract causing the diaphragm to flatten.
- These two movements cause an increase in the volume of the thorax ...
- ... and a decrease in pressure which results in atmospheric air entering.

To exhale:
- The muscles between the ribs relax allowing them to fall.
- The diaphragm muscles also relax.
- These movements cause a decrease in the volume of the thorax ...
- ... and an increase in pressure resulting in air being forced out.

Capacity For Exchanging Gases

... depends primarily on the size of a breath, and the number you take per minute. There are FIVE key terms you should understand ...

TIDAL VOLUME
- The volume of AIR you inhale or exhale with each breath is called your TIDAL VOLUME.

RESPIRATORY RATE
- How many BREATHS you take in a minute is called your RESPIRATORY RATE.

MINUTE VOLUME
- The volume of air breathed in (or out!) in one minute is called your MINUTE VOLUME.

TIDAL VOLUME x RESPIRATORY RATE = MINUTE VOLUME

- This is around 0.5L in adults at rest, but can rise to 3.0L during exercise.
- Between 8 - 15 at rest but can rise to 30+.
- 4 - 6L at rest but can rise to 90+ during extreme exercise.

VITAL CAPACITY
- Is the <u>MAXIMUM</u> amount of air you can breathe out in a forced exhalation after having a maximum possible inhalation (see the spirometer diagram opposite).

VO_2 MAX
- Is the maximum amount of oxygen your body can make use of in one minute. The fitter you are, the more efficient the alveoli become and the higher your minute volume is. This results in a higher VO_2 MAX.

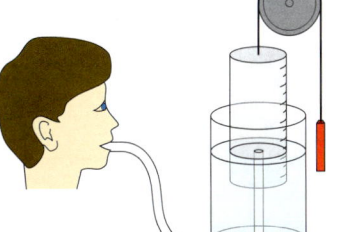

A SPIROMETER can measure tidal volume and vital capacity.

ENERGY FROM FOOD

The Human Body · 13

How Humans Obtain Energy

The Sun is the energy source for nearly every living thing on this planet. The Sun's energy is fixed by plants which form part of our food chain.

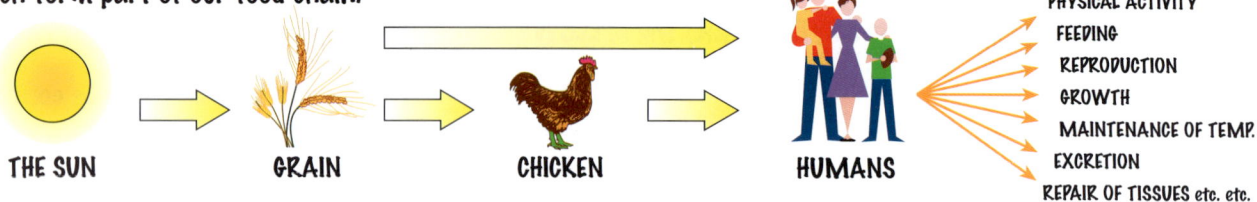

THE SUN → GRAIN → CHICKEN → HUMANS → PHYSICAL ACTIVITY, FEEDING, REPRODUCTION, GROWTH, MAINTENANCE OF TEMP., EXCRETION, REPAIR OF TISSUES etc. etc.

Making Energy Available For Physical Activity

- Carbohydrate in the form of starch from foods such as Pasta, bread and potatoes forms most of our immediate energy supply. The starch is digested to glucose molecules which then pass through the walls of the small intestine and into the blood.

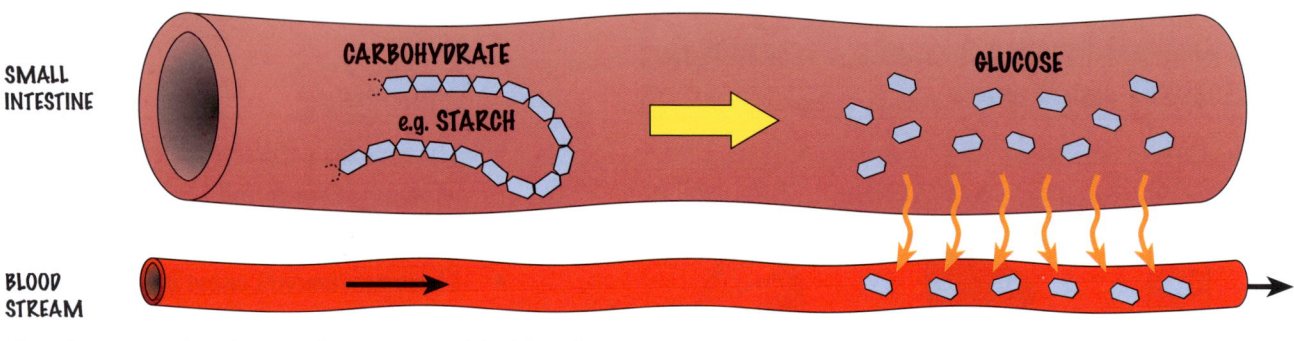

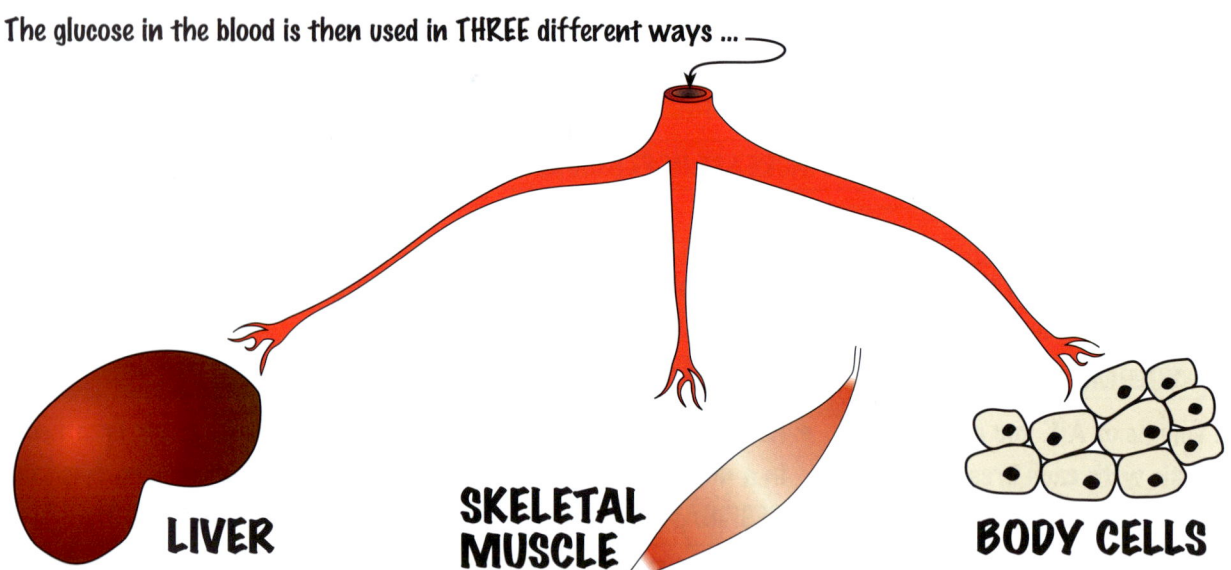

SMALL INTESTINE: CARBOHYDRATE e.g. STARCH → GLUCOSE

BLOOD STREAM

The glucose in the blood is then used in THREE different ways ...

LIVER
- The liver joins the glucose molecules up again to form GLYCOGEN which is stored and subsequently used to maintain blood sugar level.

SKELETAL MUSCLE
- The glucose is again converted to GLYCOGEN and stored in skeletal muscle for use in muscular activity. After exercise it is replenished from the blood glucose.

BODY CELLS
- Glucose diffuses easily into the cells and is used to meet the cell's energy demand via RESPIRATION.

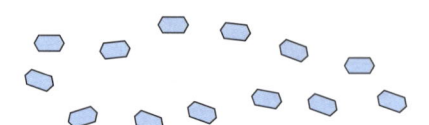

Maintaining The Balance

The glycogen in the skeletal muscles is used up during exercise, even though glucose constantly enters the muscle cells from the blood. After exercise the muscle glycogen is restored using glucose from the blood. The blood glucose then starts to fall but is immediately topped up from the reservoir in the liver.

RESPIRATION I - AEROBIC

The Human Body — 14

Providing Oxygen To Cells

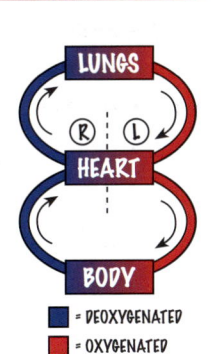

- The circulatory system carries oxygen from the lungs to all the body cells.
- This oxygen is needed in order to release the energy from glucose in aerobic respiration ...
  ... so that the working cells have enough energy to do their work.
- The rate at which oxygen is delivered to the cells depends on ...
  ... the RATE AT WHICH THE LUNGS CAN ABSORB OXYGEN, ...
  ... and the RATE AT WHICH THE HEART CAN DELIVER IT.

(Diagram: LUNGS — HEART (R/L) — BODY; blue = DEOXYGENATED, red = OXYGENATED)

Aerobic Respiration

... 'is the release of energy from the breakdown of glucose, ...
... by combining it with OXYGEN inside living cells.'

THE EQUATION: GLUCOSE + OXYGEN ⟹ CARBON DIOXIDE + WATER + ENERGY

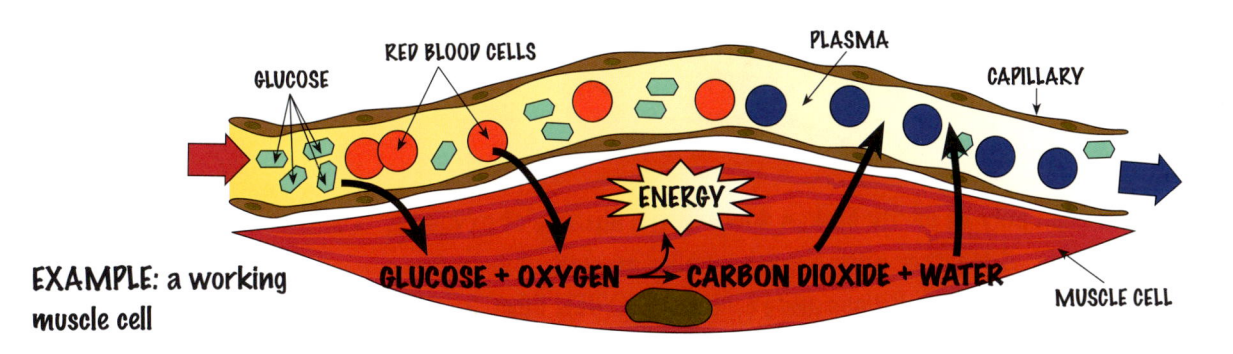

EXAMPLE: a working muscle cell

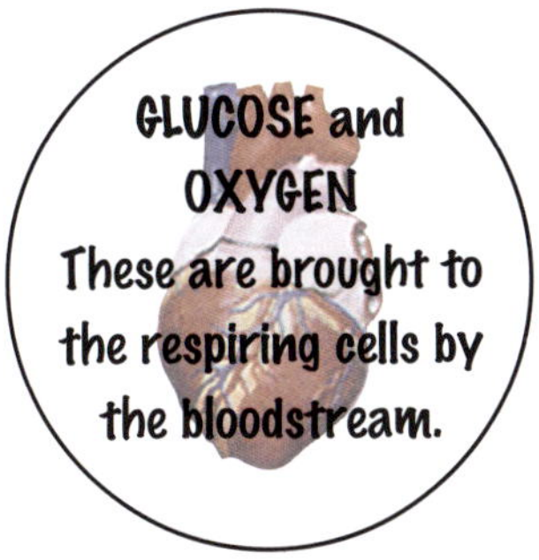

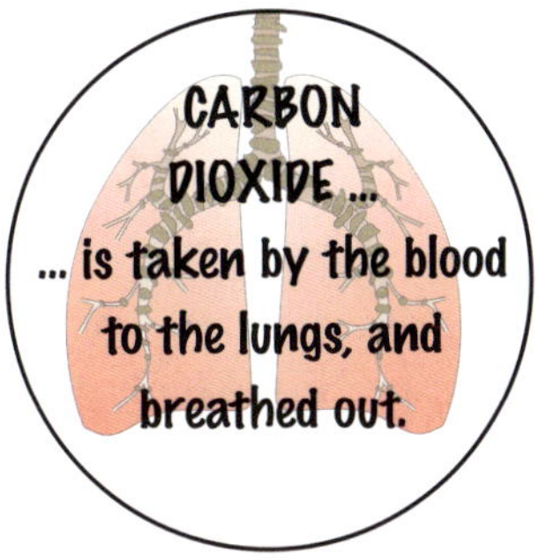

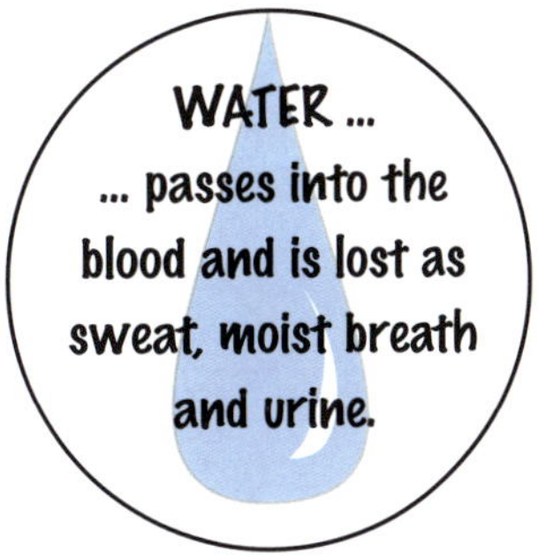

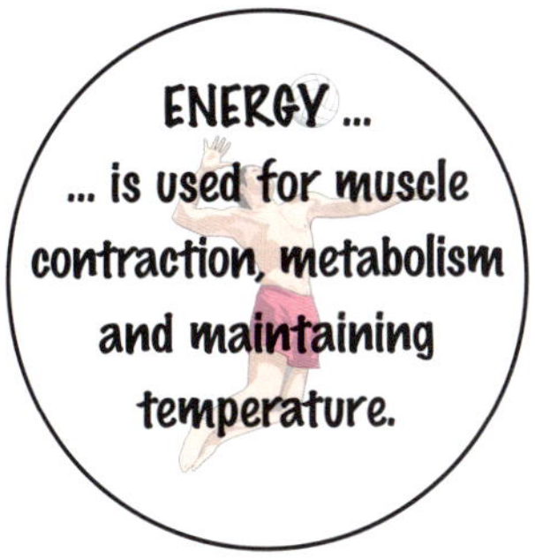

(Diagram of capillary with RED BLOOD CELLS, GLUCOSE, PLASMA feeding MUSCLE CELL: GLUCOSE + OXYGEN → CARBON DIOXIDE + WATER + ENERGY)

- **GLUCOSE and OXYGEN** — These are brought to the respiring cells by the bloodstream.
- **CARBON DIOXIDE** ... is taken by the blood to the lungs, and breathed out.
- **WATER** ... passes into the blood and is lost as sweat, moist breath and urine.
- **ENERGY** ... is used for muscle contraction, metabolism and maintaining temperature.

Some Facts About Aerobic Respiration

- This is a very efficient method of producing energy, and 1 molecule of glucose can provide twenty times as much energy as ANAEROBIC RESPIRATION (see next page).
- It occurs during normal day to day activity and accounts for our energy production up to about 60% of maximum effort.
- The drawback is that it doesn't produce energy very quickly - only about 1/3rd as quickly as ANAEROBIC.

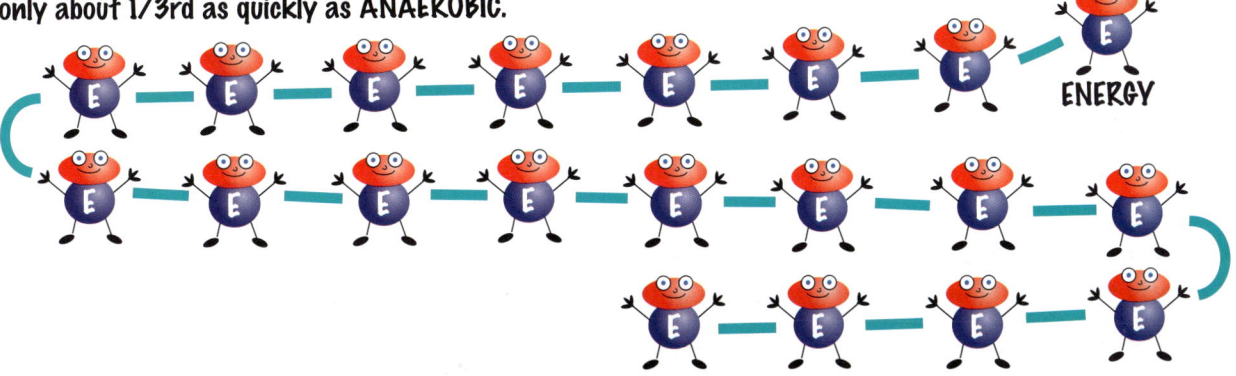

GLUCOSE   OXYGEN   "Nice and steady does it"   STEADILY → ENERGY

RESPIRATION 2 – ANAEROBIC

The Human Body — 15

Anaerobic Respiration

... is the release of a little bit of energy, <u>very quickly</u>, from the INCOMPLETE breakdown of glucose in the ABSENCE OF OXYGEN.

- This happens when the muscles need to work so hard that ...
  ... the lungs and bloodstream can't deliver enough oxygen to respire the available glucose aerobically.

THE EQUATION: **GLUCOSE ⟶ LACTIC ACID + A BIT OF ENERGY**

- **GLUCOSE** ... from the bloodstream AND GLYCOGEN in the muscles.
- **LACTIC ACID** ... accumulates in the muscles making them feel tired and 'rubbery'.
- **A BIT OF ENERGY** ... but produced quickly and used for explosive activity.

Oxygen Debt

- Because the glucose can only be partly broken down in the absence of oxygen ...
  ... LACTIC ACID is produced together with a much smaller amount of energy.
- Build up of lactic acid causes acute fatigue and results in OXYGEN DEBT ...
  ... which must be 'repaid' by continued deep breathing after exercise.

OXYGEN to repay debt + 1/5th of LACTIC ACID ⟶ CARBON DIOXIDE + WATER + ENERGY

used to convert Remaining 4/5ths of LACTIC ACID into GLUCOSE / GLYCOGEN

FATIGUE is the inability to continue exercise due to:
- LACTIC ACID build up in muscles
- DEPLETION OF GLYCOGEN STORES (in muscles/liver)

Some Facts About Anaerobic Respiration

- Anaerobic respiration is an inefficient process since it produces only 1/20th as much energy as aerobic respiration (see previous page).
- However it produces energy THREE TIMES faster and so is used during high intensity (explosive) activity over a <u>short period</u>.
- After a relatively short time, the build up of lactic acid affects the performance of the muscles and an OXYGEN DEBT is incurred.

GLUCOSE — EXPLOSIVELY ⟶ ENERGY + LACTIC ACID

Lonsdale School Revision Guides

THE NERVOUS AND HORMONAL SYSTEMS

The Human Body — 16

The NERVOUS and HORMONAL SYSTEMS allow parts of the body to communicate.

> The BRAIN is at the centre of the body's communication system. 
> - It makes sense of information from our surroundings.
> - It sends instructions to the body.

- The NERVOUS SYSTEM allows us to SEE, HEAR, MOVE and FEEL. It passes information to and from the brain using ELECTRICAL IMPULSES.

- The NERVOUS SYSTEM is similar to a telephone system.

  The Brain is like the handset. It can send and receive information.

  The Nerves are like the telephone wire, they are responsible for carrying the signal.

However ...
If there is damage to the nerves the body will not work properly.

The SPINAL CORD is the biggest collection of nerves.

Damage to the spinal cord, for example by a broken back, can leave a person paralysed and unable to move muscles in the lower body.

- The HORMONAL SYSTEM relies on chemical messengers (hormones) which are released by the brain and other hormone release sites (glands) directly into the bloodstream.

- The HORMONAL SYSTEM is an actual delivery system, similar to the postal service.

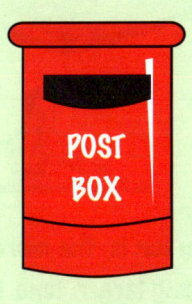

  The hormone is sent from one place and is delivered to another (the target organ) by the bloodstream. When it arrives it stimulates various changes in the body.

Hormones are very powerful chemicals. They include:

- **ADRENALIN** which prepares the body for action.

  It is released when the body perceives it is under threat, for example, before a game the release of adrenalin increases heart and respiratory rates.

- **INSULIN** which controls blood sugar.

  It is released when your blood sugar level rises. It converts blood sugar to glycogen and stores it in the liver.

Lonsdale School Revision Guides

19

ENERGY REQUIREMENTS

The Human Body — 17

The energy we transfer in our bodies comes from the food we eat. It is transferred into many different forms of energy but the two most obvious are MOVEMENT (Kinetic) ENERGY and HEAT ENERGY. Our total energy need is given by the following equation ...

TOTAL ENERGY NEED = BASAL METABOLIC RATE (BMR) + WORKING ENERGY

Basal Metabolic Rate

This is the rate of energy transfer which is just sufficient to maintain our body temperature and to keep us alive, but motionless. It is the minimum energy requirement for life and is equivalent to the use of petrol by a car that is quietly ticking over.

R.P.M. "Ticking Over"

Working Energy

This is the energy used to go about our daily business whether we are at work or play. The more active we are, the more energy we transfer and therefore the more "fuel" we need in terms of food.

The bigger, or more active a person is, the more energy they will need ... and vice versa. Consequently age is a factor, as is gender i.e. men, being larger, tend to need more energy.

Energy Balance

Energy is measured in Kilojoules or Kilocalories and it follows that if your ENERGY INTAKE is equal to the energy you transfer then your weight will remain constant. However if this isn't the case, the following may happen ...

OBESITY

... excess intake of food is stored as FAT eventually causing clinical OBESITY, and resulting in SKELETAL and JOINT problems. Excess body weight can impair performance and can slow you down. The strain on the heart can lead to heart attacks.

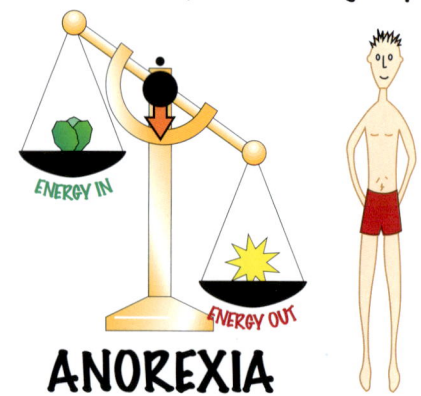

ANOREXIA

... too small an intake of food results in the use of fat reserves and severe weight loss. Ultimately protein is used as fuel resulting in ANOREXIA. Loss of muscle mass results in a less powerful performance. It can even result in death. Anorexia is often caused by a false self-image.

DIET AND NUTRITION

The Human Body — 18

A BALANCED DIET is a very important factor in maintaining good health, and there are SEVEN important components in a balanced diet ...

The Healthy Heptagon

CARBOHYDRATE
- These are broken down to glucose to provide fast-release energy.

FATS
- These contain lots of energy which can be stored for slow-release energy

VITAMINS
- Vitamin A (milk, butter and fish) healthy skin and good night vision.
- Vitamin C (citrus fruits and vegetables) helps to prevent scurvy.
- Vitamin D (milk, fish, eggs and sunshine.) It prevents rickets.

MINERALS
- Iron from liver and green vegetables prevents thyroid problems.
- Calcium from milk and cheese produces strong teeth and bones.

FIBRE
- Fibre/roughage is indigestible plant material which gives the gut something to push on, helping to avoid constipation.

WATER
- As most of the body is water we need to constantly replace that which is lost in urine, sweat and breathing, by taking in fluids.

PROTEIN
- Provides the 'fabric' for most of the soft tissues. A good protein intake is essential for growth and repair.

How Much Of Each?

It's not enough to just make sure you eat all 7 of the components above - you have to eat them in the right proportions. Vitamins and minerals are needed in only tiny amounts but the three main components are needed in very definite proportions ...

... although these proportions may change slightly under different circumstances (e.g. bodybuilding, slimming.)

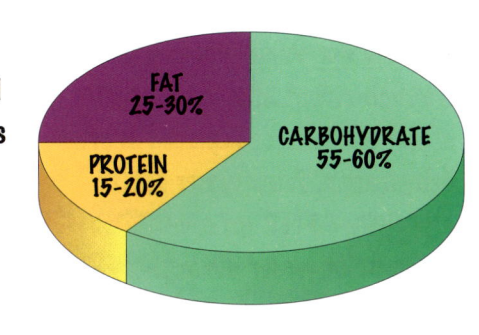

FAT 25-30%
PROTEIN 15-20%
CARBOHYDRATE 55-60%

Food Sources

Rules For A Healthy Diet

- Most **CARBOHYDRATES** should come from fruit and vegetables and some from bread, rice and pasta.
- Most **PROTEIN** should come from low fat sources such as fish, chicken, lean meat and soya. Dairy produce like cheese and eggs contain a lot of fat.
- Try to include **FAT** from olive oil and nuts instead of butter and margarine.
- Foods high in **FIBRE/ROUGHAGE** are fresh fruit and vegetables so include a lot of these in your diet.
- Check nutritional information on food labels.
- Drink lots of **WATER** especially when exercising.

Nutritional Info per 100g	
PROTEIN	4.1g
CARBOHYDRATE	61.2g
FIBRE	3.2g

SPECIAL DIETS

Special Diets

The ratio of carbohydrate, protein and fat recommended in recent years has been ...

FAT 25-30%
PROTEIN 15-20%
CARBOHYDRATE 55-60%

Although athletes will stick to the general rules for a healthy diet, some may choose to alter the ratio of carbohydrates, proteins and fat depending upon their event ...

STRENGTH EVENTS

Athletes who rely upon strength for their sport will often do a lot of weight training. In order to help their muscles grow and repair they eat more protein.

Protein is broken down into amino acids which are then restructured to form muscle protein.

WATER INTAKE

The most vital component of a competitor's diet is water. When you exercise you lose water through sweat at a much greater rate. This water needs to be replaced in order to avoid dehydration. Drink water BEFORE, DURING and especially AFTER an event. amounts of water during

ENDURANCE EVENTS

Sports people who compete in events which require a high level of endurance will often choose a diet with a higher intake of carbohydrates. This is to provide the energy for long periods of exercise.

"CARBO LOADING" (This is carbohydrate loading) Endurance athletes may change their diet in this way just before a big event ...

FIRST - They reduce their body carbohydrate stores by eating a diet consisting of protein and fat. This is done for a period of three days, a week before the event.

SECOND - For the next three days leading up to the event, they eat lots of carbohydrate and train lightly. This raises the athletes carbohydrate stores in the form of GLYCOGEN in their muscles. Hence, their muscles can work for longer.

- Regardless of the type of event in which you compete, you should never introduce something different to your diet, that you haven't used in training.

- The proportions of carbohydrate, protein and fat stated above have been fashionable for the last 20 years. More recent nutritional research has concluded that a more traditional diet, which is slightly higher in protein and lower in carbohydrate is likely to be healthier.

- REMEMBER! Eating FRESH fruit and vegetables is always best because they contain more vitamins and minerals.

REASONS FOR EXERCISE

Training And Exercise — 1

Exercise and physical recreation promote general healthiness. The World Health Organisation defines Health as ...
... "a state of complete PHYSICAL, SOCIAL and MENTAL well-being."

Physical Well-being

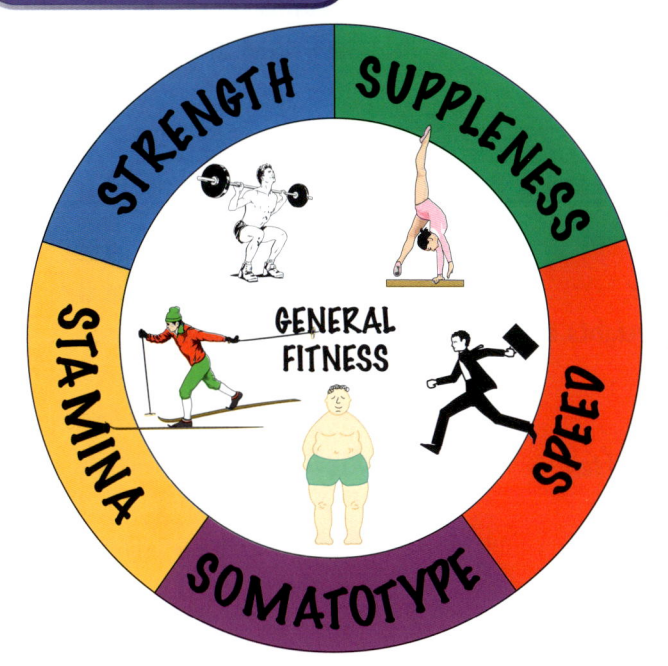

STRENGTH • SUPPLENESS • SPEED • SOMATOTYPE • STAMINA — GENERAL FITNESS

(a) PHYSICAL FITNESS

- Exercise improves general physical fitness as defined by the 5 S's (It's a bit of a cheat really as Somatotype is used instead of "Body composition!")
- These will be improved to greater or lesser degrees depending on the nature of the exercise. Suppleness, (or flexibility) becomes increasingly important with age and can limit even simple ranges of movement such as tying a lace.

(b) POSTURE

- Exercise improves your posture by improving your MUSCLE TONE. This enables you to hold your body in such a way that avoids strain on joints.
- This is particularly important for the VERTEBRAL COLUMN. Poor posture can lead to persistant back pain and ultimately time off work (see p44).

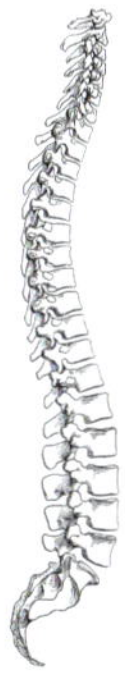

Social Well-being

- Participation in team sports promotes a sense of team spirit and comradeship.
- Taking part in any sport invariably means meeting people ...
  ... who are also interested in the same sport as you!
- Off the field activities are likely to be just as rewarding as the sport itself!
- Also, some sports carry enhanced social status ...

The captain of the school football team.

Mental Well-being

- Exercise reduces STRESS and relieves TENSION. It makes you feel more generally laid-back!
- Physical recreation can provide mental stimulation if the pursuit is challenging ...
  ... and can increase your self-confidence as you improve.
- You learn to view life in a better perspective.

THE PRINCIPLES OF TRAINING

Training And Exercise — 2

There are four guiding principles which apply to all fitness training. They are ...

1. Specificity

Training must be specific to ...

... the **SPORT** or **ACTIVITY** ...

... the **TYPE OF FITNESS** required ...

... the **PARTICULAR MUSCLE GROUPS.**

- Marathon runners do mostly ... ... ENDURANCE WORK.
- Swimmers exercise ... ... 'SWIM SPECIFIC' MUSCLES. 

2. Overload

Training must be raised to a higher level than is normal to create the extra demands to which the body will adapt. This can be done in three ways.

INCREASE THE INTENSITY ... ... by running faster, lifting heavier weights etc.

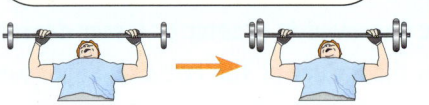

INCREASE THE FREQUENCY ... ... by training more often, 3 or 4 times a week.

INCREASE THE DURATION ... ... by training longer to prolong the demands.

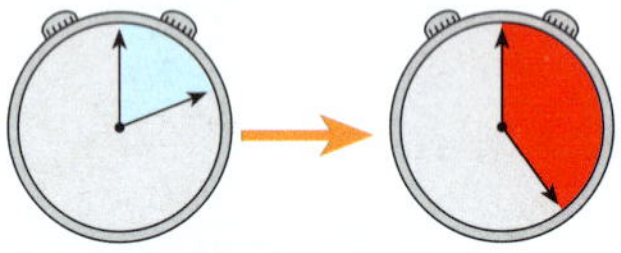

FITT is an easy way to remember the first and second guiding principles:

F – Frequency (how often you exercise)
I – Intensity (how hard you exercise)
T – Time (how long you exercise for)
T – Type (what exercises are suitable for your chosen sport)

3. Progression

As the body adapts to training it PROGRESSES to a new level of fitness.
Progress to the next level is achieved by a GRADUAL INCREASE IN INTENSITY to CREATE AN OVERLOAD.
A typical graph of LEVEL OF FITNESS against TIME would look like:

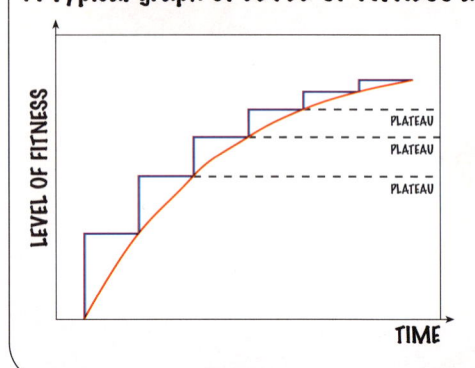

Three important points about the graph.

1. Most progress is made in the early stages.
2. At higher levels of fitness there is less progress.
3. A PLATEAU may be reached where further PROGRESSION to a higher level of fitness is difficult to achieve.

4. Reversibility

Training effects are reversible. If exercise is reduced in intensity or stopped altogether then the benefit can be quickly lost. Deterioration sets in after about one week. Strength and speed are gradually lost with muscles losing their tone and size, i.e. ATROPHY.

MUSCULAR ENDURANCE AND STRENGTH

Training And Exercise — 3

Muscular Endurance

MUSCULAR ENDURANCE is the ability of MUSCLES to CONTRACT and RELAX REPEATEDLY over a prolonged period of time AGAINST A RESISTANCE.

TWO examples of sports requiring competitors to have muscular endurance are:

CYCLING ... ... AND ... ... RUNNING

Muscular Strength

MUSCULAR STRENGTH is the amount of FORCE MUSCLES are able to EXERT AGAINST A RESISTANCE. There are THREE types of strength.

STATIC
- Maximum force versus immovable object.
- Muscle length remains constant.
- Little or no movement of limbs.

Static strength is needed in ...
... TUG OF WAR contest and a RUGBY SCRUM.
Both need to ... hold a steady position
    ... by maintaining a constant force
        ... in order to resist an opposing force.

EXPLOSIVE
- Maximum force used in one movement ...
    ... i.e. POWER.
- Combination of SPEED and FORCE.

Explosive strength is needed by an athlete in ...
... the HIGH JUMP and SHOT PUT.
Both need ... speed of movement
    ... maximum muscular effort.

DYNAMIC
- Repetitive application of force ...
- ... i.e. muscle contractions.
- It is a measure of MUSCULAR ENDURANCE.

Dynamic strength is needed in RUNNING, CYCLING and ROWING.
They all need ... maximum effort initially
    ... repeated and dynamic muscle action ...
        ... maintenance of constant speed.

The activities above all need only ONE particular type of strength.
However ... many other activities require TWO OR MORE types of strength in varying degrees.
e.g. Tennis, Rugby, Hockey, Netball.

MUSCULAR STRENGTH

Training And Exercise — 4

Improving Muscular Strength

In order to improve **STATIC STRENGTH**, **EXPLOSIVE STRENGTH** and **DYNAMIC STRENGTH** we must use the FOUR principles of training ...

- 1. SPECIFICITY • 2. OVERLOAD • 3. PROGRESSION • 4. REVERSIBILITY (see p24)

STATIC STRENGTH
Can be improved by ...
- ... using HEAVY WEIGHTS or HIGH RESISTANCE.
- ... doing a FEW REPETITIONS at a SLOW PACE.
- ... INCREASING THE RESISTANCE.

EXPLOSIVE STRENGTH
Can be improved by ...
- ... using MEDIUM to HEAVY ... ... WEIGHTS or MEDIUM RESISTANCE.
- ... doing FAST REPETITIONS.
- ... INCREASING THE RESISTANCE.

DYNAMIC STRENGTH
Can be improved by ...
- ... using LIGHT WEIGHTS ... ... or LOW RESISTANCE.
- ... doing MANY REPETITIONS.
- ... INCREASING THE DURATION or NUMBER OF REPETITIONS.

Tests For Muscular Strength

TESTING STATIC STRENGTH
- ... DYNAMOMETER ... ... which measures hand grip.

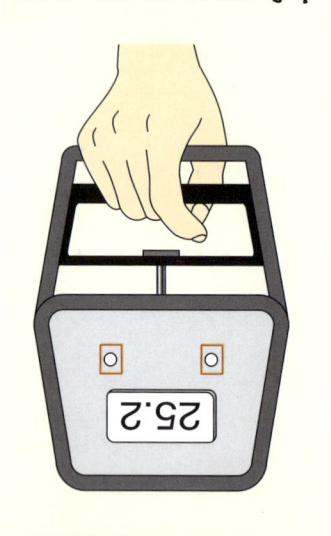

TESTING EXPLOSIVE STRENGTH
- ... VERTICAL JUMP.

TESTING DYNAMIC STRENGTH
- ... PRESS-UPS or SIT-UPS ... ... completed in 1 minute.

SPEED

Training And Exercise 5

How Speed Is Applied In Physical Activities

SPEED is the TIME TAKEN to move all or parts of the body through a SPECIFIED DISTANCE, for example ...

FOOTBALL
- Kicking the ball over a long distance, requires good leg speed, as does sprinting to get to the ball before the other side.

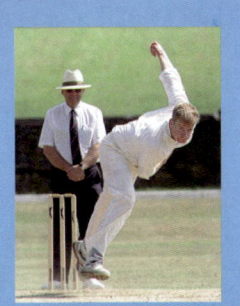

CRICKET
- Fast bowling, obviously, but fielding also requires fast arm and torso speed to throw long distances.

GOLF
- Driving the ball over a long distance requires fast arm and torso speed.

How Quickly Can The Body Move?

Speed of movement is determined by ...
... how fast the SKELETAL MUSCLES CONTRACT ...
... which is determined by MUSCLE COMPOSITION.

SLOW TWITCH MUSCLES - less powerful, slower contractions.

FAST TWITCH MUSCLES - powerful contractions produced very quickly.

So the more fast twitch fibres you have - the faster you are. The amount of fast twitch fibres the body has is GENETICALLY DETERMINED.

To improve speed you should practice the movement at a faster speed. SPECIFIC SPEED TRAINING will improve how quickly muscles can contract.

Fitness Test Designed For Testing Speed

Sprint Test
- Measure a set distance (e.g. 30, 50 or 100m) from point A to point B.
- The test is to start at point A in a stationary position and run as fast as you can to point B (running hard past point B).
- Time how long it takes to complete the test in seconds.
- If you have the equipment (e.g. timing gates), you can record the time at intervals (e.g. 5, 10, 20m) during the run to calculate acceleration and maximum running speed.

FLEXIBILITY 1

Training And Exercise — 6

What Is Flexibility?

FLEXIBILITY is the RANGE OF MOVEMENT around a JOINT. It is also known as MOBILITY or SUPPLENESS. It depends on ...

- The TYPE and STRUCTURE ... ... of the joint ... ... i.e. bone shape, ligament length.
- The LENGTH and ELASTICITY ... ... of the MUSCLES ... ... that work the joint.
- REGULAR USE and EXERCISE ... ... since joints lose their ... ... flexibility rapidly.

It is needed to ...

- PREVENT INJURY ... ... as a large range of ... ... movement reduces the risk ... ... of OVER STRETCHING.
- PREPARE FOR PERFORMANCE ... ... to loosen and relax muscles as part of a warm up routine which takes the body through a range of expected movements.

How Flexibility Enhances Performance

Flexibility is one factor that enhances the performance of a competitor. Improving their flexibility results in competitors being able to ...

... INCREASE THE RANGE OVER WHICH MUSCLES APPLY FORCE.

- BIOMECHANICAL EFFICIENCY is improved and performance is enhanced in sports such as ...

... SWIMMING for better stroke efficiency and ...
... SPRINTING for increased stride length.

... IMPROVE THE EFFECTIVENESS OF ANTAGONISTIC MUSCLES.

- COORDINATION and AGILITY is improved and performance is enhanced in sports such as ...

... FOOTBALL and HOCKEY for better passing and controlling of the ball.

... DISPLAY FLEXIBILITY BY THE EXECUTION OF MOVES AND THE HOLDING OF BALANCED POSITIONS.

- AESTHETIC BODY LINES and AGILITY is improved and moves can be executed with greater form and style in sports such as ...

... GYMNASTICS and DIVING for somersaults, twists, tucks and pikes.

FLEXIBILITY 2

Training And Exercise — 7

Exercises To Improve And Develop Flexibility

Stretching exercises should be done on a regular basis with the stretch held for at least 10 seconds working up to 30 seconds. Muscles stretch more easily after contraction and it is very important that stretching exercises are included in WARM UP and COOL DOWN routines. Stretching exercises fall into three categories.

STATIC
- The muscle is extended beyond its normal range and held for 10 to 30 seconds.
- It is then relaxed and the process repeated.

PASSIVE
- An external force is applied through a partner, couch, wall or floor to assist with the stretch. Extreme care is needed.

ACTIVE
- Rhythmical movements that imitate the activity to be undertaken.
- A warm up is needed before this exercise.

It is important to realise that ...
Stretching exercises increase the flexibility of muscles while exercises that INCREASE STRENGTH cause MUSCLES TO SHORTEN. This DECREASES THEIR FLEXIBILITY! It is therefore vital to ensure both flexibility and strength are developed to avoid any muscular imbalance.

Testing Flexibility

Common methods are ...

SIT AND REACH TEST

This measures how far you can reach relative to your toes.

THE MUSCLE TIGHTNESS TEST

Notice how flexibility can be greater on one side than the other.

Lonsdale School Revision Guides

29

AEROBIC AND ANAEROBIC TRAINING

Training And Exercise — 8

Aerobic And Anaerobic Fitness

Most physical activities require a combination of ...
- ... **AEROBIC FITNESS** which is attainable through low intensity training and is needed for endurance and 'recovery' for the removal of lactic acid. It provides a good foundation for reaching higher levels of fitness.
- ... **ANAEROBIC FITNESS** which involves higher intensity training and is needed for short, explosive bursts of activity. It requires a good foundation of aerobic fitness.

Typical fitness demands of different activities is shown below.

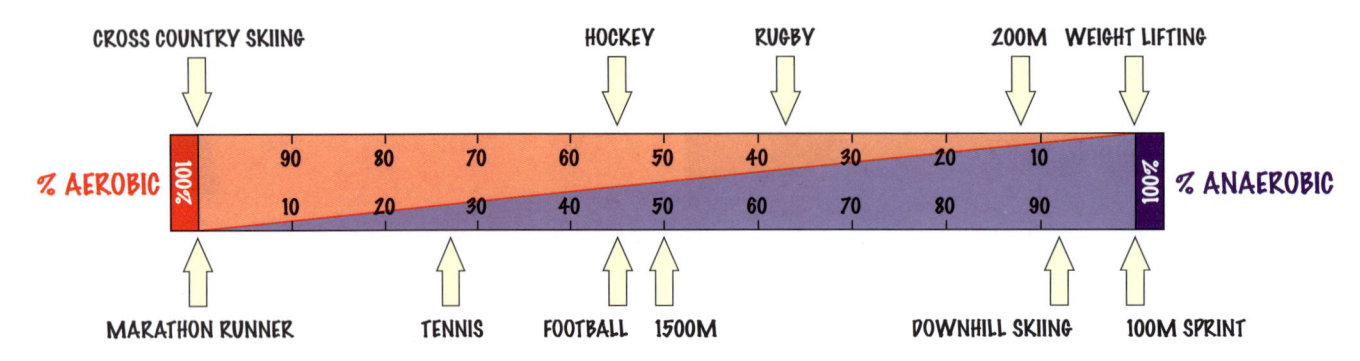

CROSS COUNTRY SKIING | HOCKEY | RUGBY | 200M | WEIGHT LIFTING

% AEROBIC 100% 90 80 70 60 50 40 30 20 10 100% % ANAEROBIC
                  10 20 30 40 50 60 70 80 90

MARATHON RUNNER | TENNIS | FOOTBALL | 1500M | DOWNHILL SKIING | 100M SPRINT

Aerobic And Anaerobic Training

AEROBIC TRAINING should ...
- ... be STRENUOUS, RHYTHMICAL and PROLONGED.
- ... be BETWEEN 60% and 85% ...
  ... of the MAXIMUM HEART RATE.
- ... use LARGE MUSCLE GROUPS.

ANAEROBIC TRAINING should ...
- ... be VERY STRENUOUS in short bursts.
- ... be AROUND or close to 85% of MAXIMUM HEART RATE.
- ... include REST and RECOVERY PERIODS.
- ... be undertaken with CAUTION.

The graph below shows the HEART RATE (H.R.) ZONE required for an individual to be training aerobically and anaerobically. The thresholds are the minimum heart rates required by an individual to benefit from the respective exercise types.

- The "age predicted maximums" are based on '220 minus the age in years' and can only be used as a guideline between aerobic and anaerobic.
- Note the region of overlap.
- The figures of 60% and 85% are generalisations and vary from individual to individual.

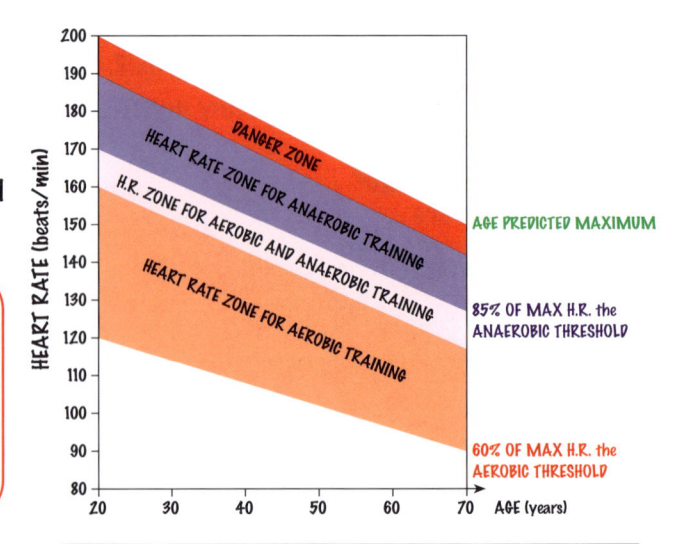

HEALTH WARNING

Training close to one's maximum heart rate should be done with caution and medical advice should be sought by people who are starting training after a long period of inactivity.

Graph: HEART RATE (beats/min) vs AGE (years). Shows DANGER ZONE, HEART RATE ZONE FOR ANAEROBIC TRAINING, H.R. ZONE FOR AEROBIC AND ANAEROBIC TRAINING, HEART RATE ZONE FOR AEROBIC TRAINING. Lines: AGE PREDICTED MAXIMUM, 85% OF MAX H.R. the ANAEROBIC THRESHOLD, 60% OF MAX H.R. the AEROBIC THRESHOLD.

AEROBIC TRAINING AFFECTS THE BODY by ...
- ... raising the AEROBIC THRESHOLD.
- ... improving ENDURANCE and CARDIOVASCULAR FITNESS.
- ... increasing LUNG CAPACITY.

ANAEROBIC TRAINING AFFECTS THE BODY by ...
- ... raising the ANAEROBIC THRESHOLD.
- ... improving MUSCULAR STRENGTH.
- ... improving LACTIC ACID TOLERANCE.

SPECIFIC TRAINING METHODS 1

Training And Exercise — 9

Training Methods

There are a variety of training methods which can be used to benefit most training programmes. The FIVE common ones are ...

- WEIGHT TRAINING
- CIRCUIT TRAINING
- INTERVAL TRAINING
- FARTLEK TRAINING
- CONTINUOUS TRAINING

All of them train both the AEROBIC and ANAEROBIC systems. The training intensity of each method can be modified to increase the gains for either type of fitness. Typical values could be ...

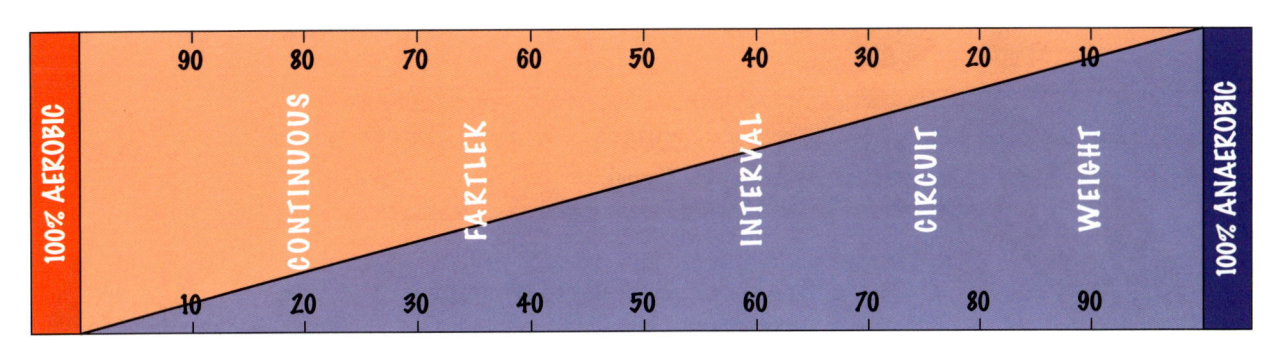

100% AEROBIC	90	80	70	60	50	40	30	20	10	100% ANAEROBIC
			CONTINUOUS	FARTLEK		INTERVAL		CIRCUIT	WEIGHT	
	10	20	30	40	50	60	70	80	90	

Each method consists of exercises or activities which may be organised into:

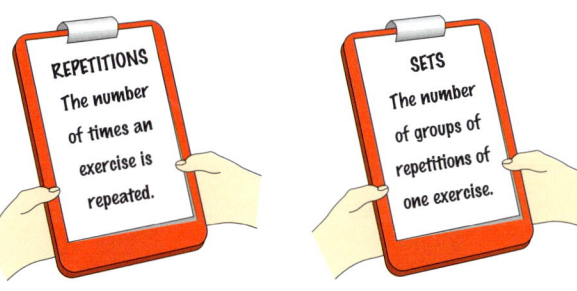

REPETITIONS — The number of times an exercise is repeated.

SETS — The number of groups of repetitions of one exercise.

Weight Training

Weight training involves a series of exercises where each one focuses on a specific muscle group in the body.

All of these exercises involve the overcoming of a RESISTANCE or LOAD by the use of a MACHINE or FREE WEIGHTS.

REPETITIONS AND SETS

These depend on whether a person is attempting to build up STRENGTH or ENDURANCE. Typical programmes could be ...

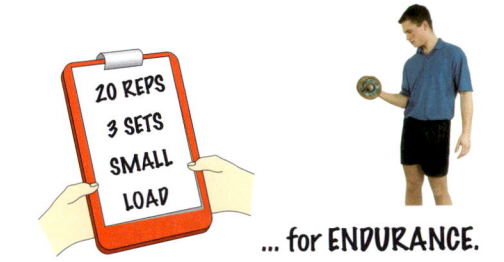

- 10 REPS, 3 SETS, LARGE LOAD ... for STRENGTH.
- 20 REPS, 3 SETS, SMALL LOAD ... for ENDURANCE.

EFFECT OF WEIGHT TRAINING ON THE BODY

- It improves ... MUSCULAR STRENGTH, ENDURANCE, TONE, POSTURE
- It increases ... MUSCULAR SIZE, BONE DENSITY, METABOLIC RATE

SPECIFIC TRAINING METHODS 2

Training And Exercise — 10

Circuit Training

Circuit training involves a series of exercises or activities, with each one taking place at a different STATION. Each station involves an exercise aimed at a specific muscle group in the body.

The exercises are arranged so that ...

- ... MUSCLE GROUPS ALTERNATE between work and recovery, to allow lactic acid dispersal.
- ... OPPOSING MUSCLE GROUPS are worked for balanced strength distribution.

SIT-UPS (Abdominals) → SQUATS (Legs) → PRESS-UPS (Arms) → STAR JUMPS (Legs) → BACK RAISER (Dorsal and Hamstrings) → SQUAT THRUSTS (Abdominals) → PULL-UPS (Arms) → SHUTTLE RUNS (Legs)

Circuits can be designed to improve ...
- Fitness (aerobic and anaerobic).
- Strength and Endurance.
- Sport specific actions.
- General muscle tone.
- Personal targets.

REPETITIONS AND SETS

Circuits can be organised on the basis of TIME or REPETITION and may include REST INTERVALS or they could be NON-STOP. A typical programme could be ...

THREE CIRCUITS. ONE SET OF TEN REPS AT EACH STATION NON-STOP!

EFFECT OF CIRCUIT TRAINING ON THE BODY

- It improves ... GENERAL MUSCULAR STRENGTH, ENDURANCE, MUSCLE TONE, POSTURE, SKILL LEVELS
- It increases ... BONE DENSITY, METABOLIC RATE and decreases ... BODY FAT %

SPECIFIC TRAINING METHODS 3

Training And Exercise — 11

Interval Training

Interval training involves ALTERNATING between FIXED PERIODS OF EXERCISE and FIXED PERIODS OF REST (or light exercise) for recovery. Careful planning is needed to match the duration and intensity of exercise and recovery with the level of fitness of the individual.

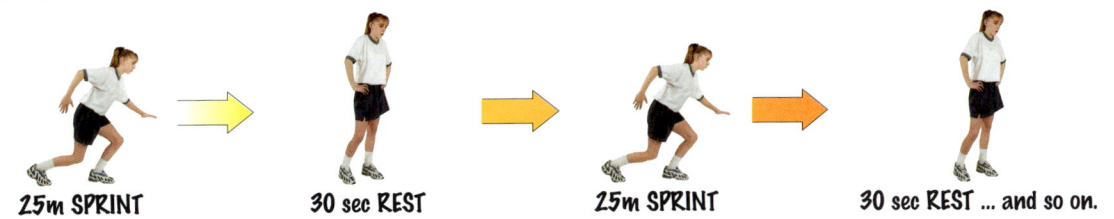

25m SPRINT → 30 sec REST → 25m SPRINT → 30 sec REST ... and so on.

Interval training is effective for most team sports and is an APPROPRIATE method of training for running and swimming.

Fartlek Training

Fartlek Training is very similar to interval training except that the INTENSITY and TYPE OF EXERCISE ARE VARIED through changes in pace, terrain and style. There are no fixed amounts of each component and a programme can be planned to suit the level of fitness of the individual.

10 min JOG → 100m WALK → 50m SPRINT → 2 min REST → 5 min JOG ... and so on.

Fartlek Training is effective for many sports including running, cycling and swimming.

EFFECT OF INTERVAL AND FARTLEK TRAINING ON THE BODY

Both have similar effects which depend on the intensity and variation of exercise, but generally ...

- They improve ... **AEROBIC AND ANAEROBIC FITNESS**
- They increase ... **METABOLIC RATE**
- They decrease ... **BODY FAT %**

Continuous Training

Continuous Training involves LONG, SLOW, DISTANCE EXERCISE (LSD) at a CONSTANT RATE WITHOUT REST. Training at first should be at 60% maximum Heart Rate progressing to 85% maximum Heart Rate as fitness improves and the distance involved increases to beyond competition distance.

EFFECT OF CONTINUOUS TRAINING ON THE BODY

- It improves ... **AEROBIC FITNESS**
- It increases ... **METABOLIC RATE** and decreases ... **BODY FAT %**

Pressure Training

Unlike the other training methods, pressure training involves a COMBINATION OF SKILLS AND FITNESS. A skill is continually performed as you become more and more tired. With practice the skill level can be improved with increasing tiredness. A footballer or a basketball player may practice ...

... dribbling and shooting ...
   ... over a set distance, ...
      ... a set number of times, ...
         ... in a set time.

This training is beneficial as it can represent the pressure they can expect to experience in an actual game.

Lonsdale School Revision Guides

TRAINING REQUIREMENTS FOR SPORT

Training And Exercise 12

Seasonal Sport

Many sports take place SEASONALLY and may be classed as SUMMER or WINTER activities. Hockey, Netball, Rugby, Football, Cricket and Rounders are all examples of seasonal sports. These activities have a CLOSED or OFF SEASON ...

... for REST and RECUPERATION.

- PLAYING SEASON, 30-36 WEEKS
- CLOSED SEASON FOR REST AND RECUPERATION, 6-10 WEEKS
- OUT OF SEASON, 4-6 WEEKS TRAINING
- PRE-SEASON, 4-6 WEEKS TRAINING

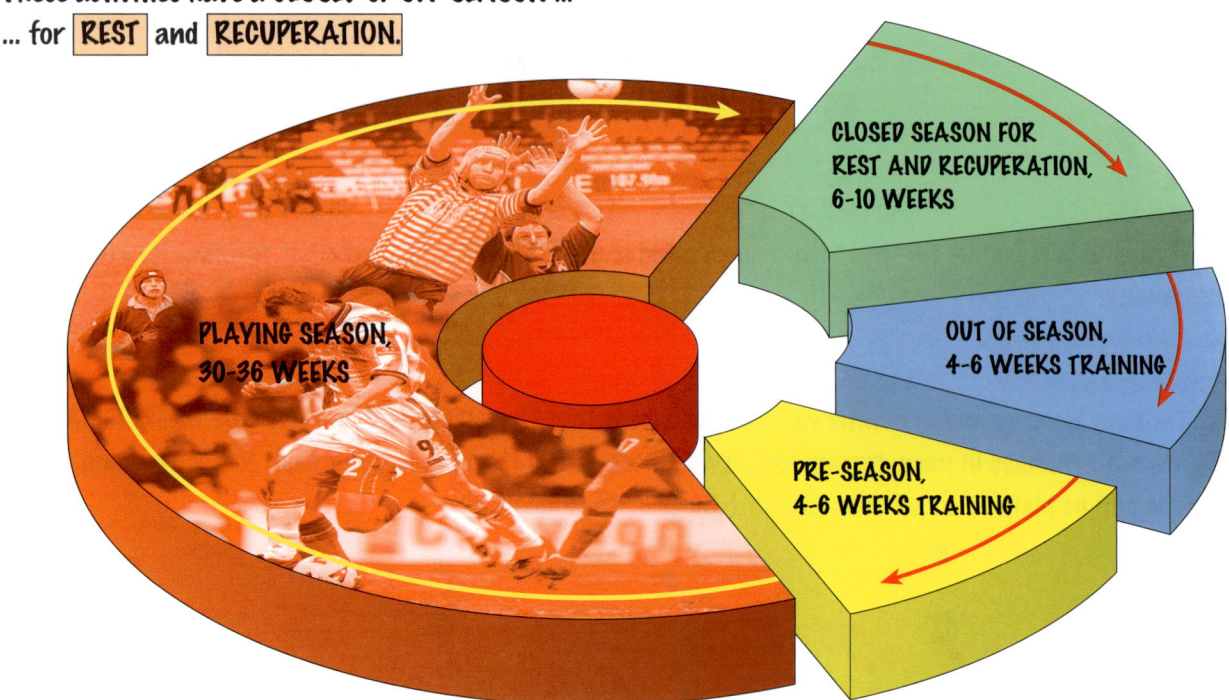

- Complete break.
- Recovery from injuries.
- Recreation and relaxation in other sports or activities.

- Light training with gradual build up to a good level of aerobic fitness.
- Light skills training with non-competitive games.

- High intensity interval and weights training.
- Flexibility and 'pressure' skills training.
- Practice matches.

- Playing once or twice a week.
- Maintenance and light weight training.
- Speed work.
- Quality rest and appropriate diet.

'All Year Round' Sports

Some sports have become 'ALL YEAR ROUND' activities with specific training requirements. Field and Track Athletes and Tennis players participate in INDOOR and OUTDOOR EVENTS throughout the year, around the world. In order to perform to their maximum potential they need to undergo ...

... WARM WEATHER AND ALTITUDE TRAINING

- Elite athletes and players train abroad in warm climates or at altitude to enhance performance. This option depends on funding and financial support being available.

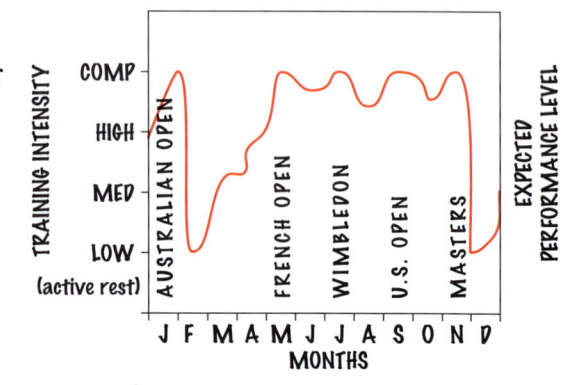

... PERIODISATION

- Training programmes are planned to achieve PEAKS at certain times throughout the year.

LONG TERM EFFECTS OF TRAINING

Training And Exercise — 13

Long term training causes the body to adapt to the increased load placed upon it by the training. Various parts of the body start to show changes ...

The Circulatory System

a) The HEART

- The heart becomes BIGGER and its walls become THICKER (they're muscles remember!).
- The coronary arteries become better at supplying the heart with blood.
- It is able to pump more blood per min ...
- ... and is therefore capable of higher HEART RATE, STROKE VOLUME AND MINUTE VOLUME.

The heart needs less beats per minute to supply the body with blood when at rest. Resting heart rate is therefore lower when you are fit. Good athletes have resting heart rates of around 50 b.p.m.

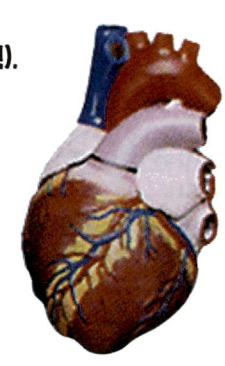

The Red Blood Cells

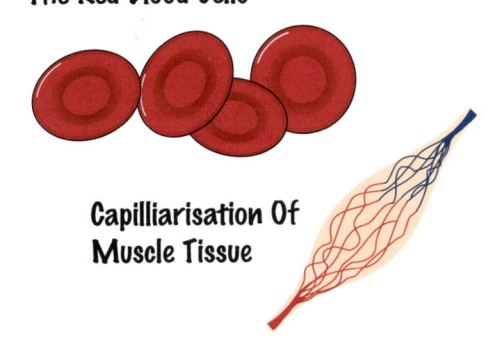

b) The BLOOD and CIRCULATION

- The number of RED BLOOD CELLS increases to cope with the demands of carrying extra oxygen.
- The capillary networks in muscles start to grow more and more branches and are therefore able to transport more blood.

ALTITUDE TRAINING has this effect on the body, a fact used by many athletes to improve their fitness capacity before important events.

Capilliarisation Of Muscle Tissue

The Respiratory System

- The diaphragm and intercostal muscles become stronger ...
  ... which increases the maximum lung volume.
  (VITAL CAPACITY INCREASES.)
- This allows greater gas exchange with each breath.
- There is an increase in the size of the capillary networks around the alveoli which means ...
- ... increased blood supply and more efficient gas exchange.

Endurance athletes work hard to specifically improve their circulatory and respiratory systems.

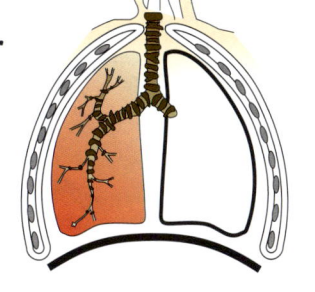

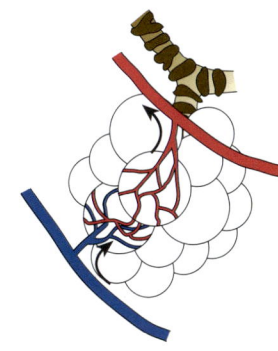

The Skeletal And Muscle Systems

- The muscles and their associated capillaries become more efficient at exchanging materials (e.g. CO_2 and O_2).
- The muscle cells themselves use the available oxygen more efficiently ...
  ... which means they can contract for longer and do more work.
- These two facts mean that the VO_2 MAX of the body is increased meaning that your body can transfer energy more quickly and is therefore more powerful (power is the rate of transferring energy).
- Muscles may or may not get bigger depending upon the type of training you do (see p.26).
- Tendons, ligaments and bones do get stronger to cope with the increased load ...
  ... and cartilage may increase to cope with impact (particularly in the knees).

Sprinters, throwers and lifters work hard to specifically improve their explosive strength.

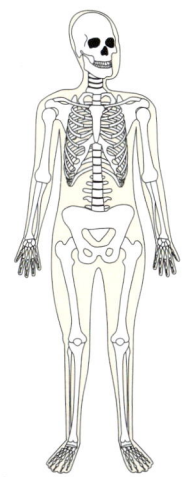

Lonsdale School Revision Guides

THE BODY'S RESPONSE TO EXERCISE

Training And Exercise 14

Cardiovascular System

- The heart rate increases with exercise (see p.13).
- ... and the stroke volume increases with severe exercise (see p.13).
- These both increase the cardiac output (see p.13).
- Blood now flows faster and is diverted to the working muscles ... ... due to VASODILATION in the vessels leading to the muscles.
- This vasodilation helps to prevent the blood pressure from rising to too high a level.

RESULT:
- THE SYSTEM NOW DELIVERS MORE OXYGEN, ...
- ... AND MORE GLUCOSE TO THE WORKING MUSCLES,
- ... AND REMOVES CARBON DIOXIDE FROM THEM MUCH MORE QUICKLY.

Cardiorespiratory System

- The respiratory rate increases with exercise (see p.15) ...
- ... and the tidal volume increases with exercise (see p.15).
- These both increase the minute volume (see p.15).
- The intercostal muscles and the diaphragm ...
- ... are responsible for these increases.

RESULT:
- OXYGEN FROM THE ATMOSPHERE, AND CARBON DIOXIDE IN THE LUNGS ARE EXCHANGED MORE RAPIDLY. THIS RESULTS IN GREATER (AND FASTER) OXYGENATION OF THE BLOOD.

Respiration In The Muscle Cells

- Increased muscle contraction means that more energy is needed ...
- ... so respiration in the muscle cells increases (see p.17 and 18), using oxygen and glucose.
- This means that lots more carbon dioxide is produced (and some lactic acid!) ...
- ... and because most of the energy produced is wasted as heat, the body starts to warm up and its temperature starts to rise.

RESULT:
- OXYGEN USED UP QUICKLY BY THE CELLS.
- GLUCOSE USED UP QUICKLY BY THE CELLS.
- LOTS OF CARBON DIOXIDE PRODUCED.
- SOME LACTIC ACID PRODUCED. LOTS OF HEAT PRODUCED.

Cooling Effect Of The Skin

- Blood vessels just beneath the skin open up (VASODILATE) to allow blood to pass close to the surface and lose heat. This causes the skin to flush.
- Sweat is produced by the sweat glands and then evaporates taking heat energy away from the skin.

RESULT:
- VASODILATION OF SKIN CAPILLARIES AND EVAPORATION OF SWEAT CAUSES THE BODY TO LOSE HEAT AND MAINTAIN NORMAL TEMPERATURE.

The Effects Of Exercise On:

❶ A TRAINED ATHLETE: maintains high fitness levels; fine tunes motor skills; enables peak performance
❷ AN AVERAGE PERFORMER: maintains health and fitness; facilitates the reaching of higher levels of fitness and performance.
❸ AN UNFIT PERFORMER: allows improved levels of fitness and health - rapid at first; lowers resting heart rate and blood pressure; improves sleep patterns and general physical and mental well-being.

TEMPERATURE REGULATION AND WATER BALANCE — Training And Exercise — 15

Temperature Regulation

- The CORE TEMPERATURE of the body is maintained at around 37°C due to the ...
  ... monitoring and control of the THERMOREGULATORY CENTRE in the brain.

CORE TEMP. TOO HIGH → THERMOREGULATORY CENTRE ← **CORE TEMP. TOO LOW**

- BLOOD VESSELS IN SKIN VASODILATE (become wider) CAUSING GREATER HEAT LOSS BY RADIATION.
- SWEAT GLANDS RELEASE SWEAT WHICH CAUSES COOLING, BY EVAPORATION.

- BLOOD VESSELS IN SKIN VASOCONSTRICT (become narrower) REDUCING HEAT LOSS BY RADIATION.
- MUSCLES START TO 'SHIVER' CAUSING HEAT ENERGY TO BE RELEASED VIA RESPIRATION IN CELLS.

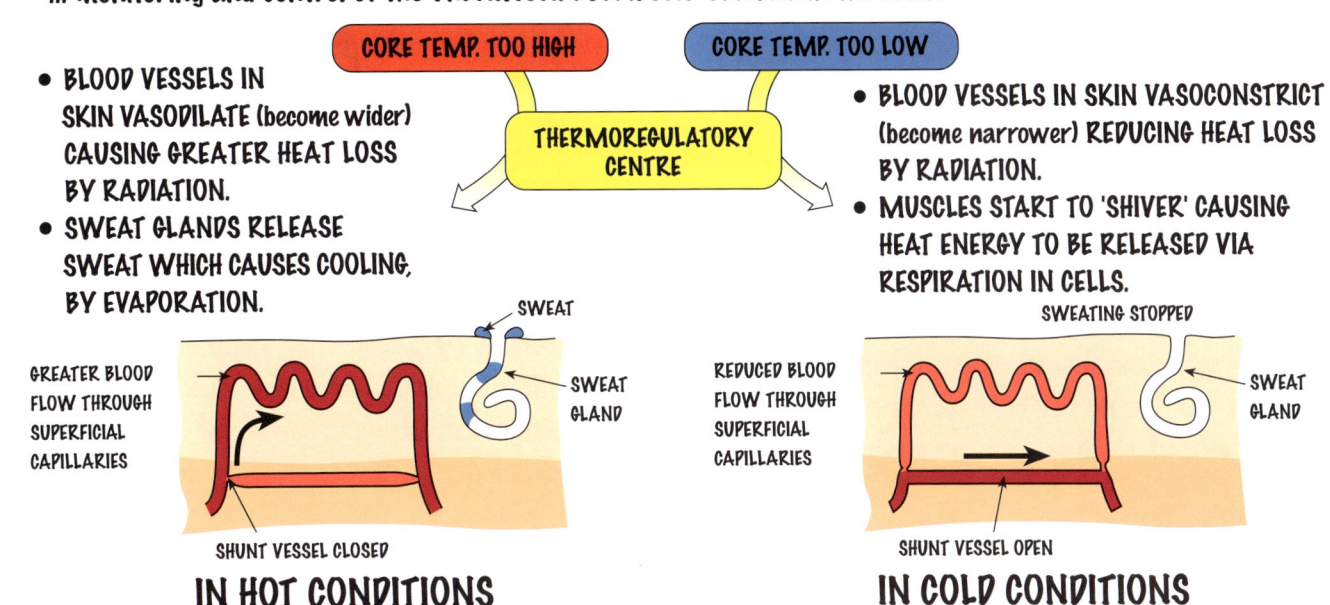

IN HOT CONDITIONS: GREATER BLOOD FLOW THROUGH SUPERFICIAL CAPILLARIES — SWEAT — SWEAT GLAND — SHUNT VESSEL CLOSED

IN COLD CONDITIONS: REDUCED BLOOD FLOW THROUGH SUPERFICIAL CAPILLARIES — SWEATING STOPPED — SWEAT GLAND — SHUNT VESSEL OPEN

Control Of Water Balance

- Of all the items in the diet, the daily intake of water is the most important.
- Humans can survive for only a few days without water because ...
  ... water makes up 70% of the body's weight and is being continually lost.

GAIN
- FLUID INTAKE
- WATER IN FOOD
- WATER FROM RESPIRATION
- 3 LITRES/DAY

LOSS
- THROUGH URINE
- THROUGH SKIN
- THROUGH BREATHING
- THROUGH FAECES
- 3 LITRES/DAY

- The amount of urine produced is adjusted to maintain the water balance ...

- If you have drunk too much you will provide a large quantity of dilute urine.

- If you are dehydrated you will produce a small quantity of concentrated urine.

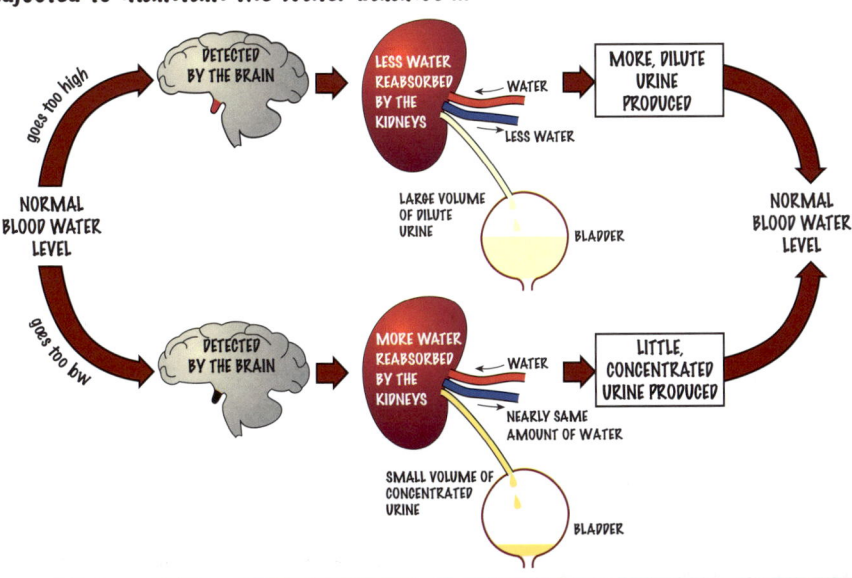

NORMAL BLOOD WATER LEVEL → goes too high → DETECTED BY THE BRAIN → LESS WATER REABSORBED BY THE KIDNEYS → WATER / LESS WATER → MORE, DILUTE URINE PRODUCED → LARGE VOLUME OF DILUTE URINE → BLADDER → NORMAL BLOOD WATER LEVEL

goes too low → DETECTED BY THE BRAIN → MORE WATER REABSORBED BY THE KIDNEYS → WATER / NEARLY SAME AMOUNT OF WATER → LITTLE, CONCENTRATED URINE PRODUCED → SMALL VOLUME OF CONCENTRATED URINE → BLADDER

Lonsdale School Revision Guides

FITNESS TESTING

Training And Exercise — 16

The Multi-stage Fitness Test

- The subject runs a distance of 20m, placing his foot over a line marked by a cone at each end.
  The subject must complete each length between the sound of two bleeps. The bleeps come at progressively shorter intervals so the subject must increase their speed, until they can no longer keep pace.
  There are 25 levels to this test.

The test measures your VO_2 max. The higher this is the fitter you are.

The Cooper Test

- The subject warms up, then at the sound of a whistle, he must run around a track for a period of 12 minutes, aiming to run as far as he can.

  At the end of this time the distance travelled is calculated to the nearest 100m.

The test also measures your VO_2 max. The further you run the fitter you are.

The Harvard Step Test

- The subject records his resting pulse rate. He then steps up and down off a 50cm high step or bench for 5 minutes at a rate of 30 steps per minute. The subject rests for one minute and then takes his pulse for 15 seconds. To find out his score, the subject calculates:

$$\frac{\text{LENGTH OF EXERCISE IN SECONDS} \times 100}{5.5 \times \text{PULSE}}$$

The test measures your cardiovascular fitness. The higher the score, the fitter you are.

The Cycle Ergometer Test

- The subject warms up then pedals for 5 minutes, setting the load according to whether they are male or female.

  The subject's pulse is recorded for 15 seconds, twenty seconds before the time is up.

The lower your active pulse rate is, the fitter you are.

- These FOUR tests all measure your aerobic fitness.

- Aerobic fitness is a reflection of how fast your heart and lungs are able to deliver oxygen to your muscles.

- Aerobic fitness is tested to see how an athlete's fitness is improving. Athletes should have a low pulse rate and should be very efficient at getting oxygen to their muscles.

TESTING SPECIFIC FITNESS

Agility – The Compass Run

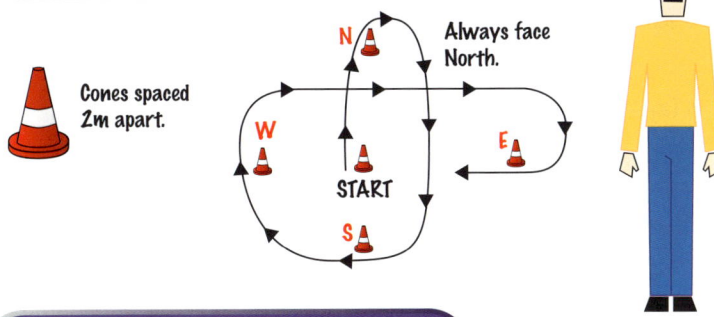

Cones spaced 2m apart.

Always face North.

Starting from the left of the centre cone, run around each cone whilst FACING NORTH AT ALL TIMES. You must circle the centre cone after each shuttle. The clock stops when you have circled the centre cone for the last time.

Balance – The Stork Stand

The test starts when you have taken position. Hands outstretched, standing on one foot with the other foot on your other knee.

SHUT YOUR EYES
Time how long before you lose balance or open your eyes.

Hands held at shoulder height out in front of yourself.

Opposite foot positioned at the side of your standing leg's knee.

Balance on your preferred foot.

Coordination – Ball Bounce Test

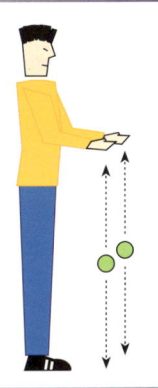

Bounce two tennis balls at the same time

Catch them with your palm facing downwards

This test begins when you start to bounce both tennis balls at the same time.

Continue bouncing the balls as many times as possible without making a mistake.

The test finishes when you make a mistake.

Reaction Time – Ruler Drop Test

Ask a partner to hold a 30 cm ruler out in front of them. Position your index finger and thumb next to the 0cm mark without actually touching the ruler. Your partner then drops the ruler without giving you any notice.
THE CLOSER TO THE 0cm MARK YOU CAN CATCH THE RULER THE FASTER YOUR REACTION TIME IS.

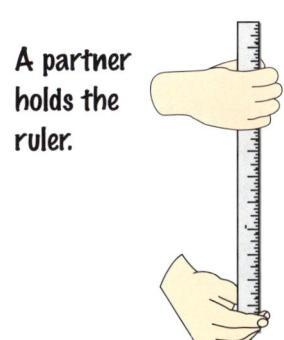

A partner holds the ruler.

Put your own hand by the 0cm mark without touching the ruler.

Power – Sergeant Jump

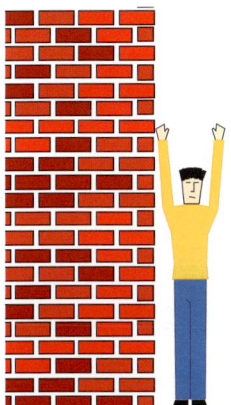

Stand beside a wall and keep your legs and feet flat on the floor. Reach straight above your head.
Make a chalk mark at the highest point you can reach.

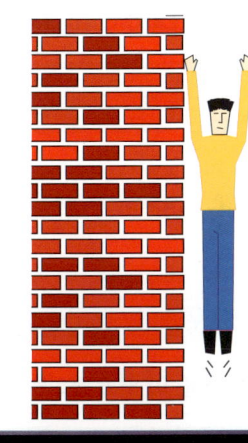

Jump as high as possible making a second chalk mark at the highest point.

The distance between the two chalk marks gives you a score for your EXPLOSIVE STRENGTH.

PREVENTION OF INJURY

Aspects Of Sport — 1

Warming Up

- A warm up prepares the body for the activity it's about to undertake ...

PHASE 1: Steady jogging ... 10 MINUTES (approx.)

... warms up the muscles to their "working" temperature, and you start to sweat.

... increases the heart rate, ideally to around 120/140 beats/minute.

... reduces stiffness in joints, allowing greater range of movement.

PHASE 2: Stretching ... 10 MINUTES (approx.)

... each stretch should be held for at least 10 seconds.

... your muscles must be warm before you start stretching.

... try to ensure that you stretch each of the relevant muscle groups in turn.

... cold muscles are like cold chewing gum and can snap easily; so be careful. Keep jogging between stretches.

PHASE 3: Mental preparation ...

Practice some of the things you're going to be doing when competition begins ...

... passing, receiving, sprint starts and sharp changes of direction may help to prepare your body for the tasks it is about to face.

Give yourself time to think about what you want to achieve. Try to become totally focused and in the right state of mind.

Maintain light jogging and gentle stretching in between the more specific activities.

Warming Down

This is the transition phase between exercise and rest, and just as you shouldn't go from rest to strenuous activity, neither should you do the opposite. The 3 main reasons for "warming down" are:-

1. Your heart rate and respiration rate return GENTLY back to normal.
2. LACTIC ACID and other waste products are removed from your muscles.
3. It helps to prevent muscle SORENESS and aids recovery.

- Basically do light jogging and gentle stretching of the main muscle groups that you used.

FOOTWEAR FOR SPORT

Aspects Of Sport — 2

Sports Shoes

Ideally sports shoes should be designed ...

- ... to PROVIDE SUPPORT to the ARCHES OF THE FEET.
- ... to CUSHION the ANKLE JOINT when impact is made with the ground during activities such as running and jumping.

Basic Rules For Buying Sports Shoes

Forget the hype, forget the style just ...

- ... buy the best you can afford. Remember "Value is a measure of what you get for the price you pay."
- ... make sure they fit properly and can do the job. High back shoes can cause achilles' tendon damage - so think on.

Specialist Sporting Footwear

Different sports nearly all require the participants to wear specialist footwear in order to compete at their best.

Cricketers wear footwear with spikes or rubber soles.

Golfers wear footwear with spikes or rubber soles.

Track runners wear spikes. Road runners wear footwear with rubber soles.

Rugby players and Footballers wear boots with studs.

Looking After Your Footwear

Unless you've got money to burn you should take good care of all your specialist equipment. Footwear in particular needs some time and effort spent on it if you are to (a) make them last and (b) get the best use out of them. Always allow your footwear to dry naturally. Don't stick them on top of a radiator or in an airing cupboard. If they have got particularly wet, pack them with newspaper to maintain their shape. When they have dried brush them with a stiff brush to remove dirt etc. and then treat them with a suitable application e.g. dubbin, polish, whitener etc. etc.

Lonsdale School Revision Guides

PLAYING SAFE

Aspects Of Sport — 3

Safety Considerations

It is important that ALL SAFETY CONSIDERATIONS are observed and applied before, during and after any practical activity.

All practical activities involve risk which can be greatly reduced by the use of common sense and by showing respect for the following considerations.

- ALL KIT AND EQUIPMENT IN GOOD CONDITION
- APPROPRIATE WARM UP BEFORE ACTIVITY
- PLAYING SURFACE IN A GOOD AND SAFE CONDITION
- INSTRUCTIONS ARE FOLLOWED
- CORRECT TECHNIQUE IS USED
- RULES ARE OBEYED

Considerations Appropriate To Different Activities

GYMNASTIC ACTIVITIES
- Floor mats in good condition.
- Supervising staff are qualified.
- Use of spotters.
- No overhanging beams.
- Use of magnesium carbonate.
- No jewellery worn & no baggy clothes.
- When lifting gymnastic equipment it is important that you keep ...
  ... your knees bent, ...
  ... a straight back ...
  ... and head up.
  This will protect your vertebral column.

GAME ACTIVITIES
- Shin pads
- Face mask/helmet
- Gum shield
- Batting/goalkeeper's gloves ...
  ... should be worn in appropriate invasion/striking games.
- Goggles.
- Secure net/posts.
- Clear playing area ...
  ... are needed in appropriate net/wall games.

ATHLETIC ACTIVITIES
- Well-conditioned, soft landing mats need placing in appropriate jumping areas.
- Rake is removed from pit ...
  ... before long jump and triple jump.
- Activity in throwing events takes place only when told to do so.
- Use warning sounds to indicate throwing events are taking place.
- No running to collect a thrown javelin.
- Always stay behind the thrower.

OUTDOOR EDUCATION
- Beware of extreme weather.
- Route Plan
- Take emergency food supplies on long walks/expeditions.
- Check kit with care.
- Ensure someone knows where you are going and when you will be back.

SWIMMING
- No running on poolside.
- Check depth of water ...
  ... before going in.
- No jumping in.
- Keep to one's depth.

DANCE
- Floor mats in good condition.
- Warm up needed ...
  ... to avoid injury.
- No jewellery worn.
- Appropriate clothing worn.

OTHER ACTIVITIES
- Follow the rules set by the Governing Body.
- Be aware of potential risks.
- Always be responsible for your own safety.
- Teacher's/Coach's instructions must always be followed.

PERSONAL HYGIENE

Aspects Of Sport — 4

Personal Hygiene

Personal hygiene is an essential consideration for any athlete. It helps to keep you healthy. The things to consider are.

The body SWEATS when you exercise, so after exercising you need to wash to remove bacteria and body odour.

A DEODORANT will disguise the smell of body odour, but it won't remove bacteria.

ANTIPERSPIRANTS prevent the body from sweating, and so shouldn't be used before exercise as the body sweats in order to regulate body temperature.

When you exercise LONG HAIR should be tied back to prevent ...
- ... your VISION becoming restricted
- ... your hair being pulled accidentally or deliberately

TEETH which should be clean of course!
May need PROTECTING with a gum SHIELD.
Nails should be kept clean and short to prevent SCRATCHING or becoming DAMAGED.

It is also important to keep CLOTHES CLEAN as they absorb sweat and allow bacteria to breed.

Footcare

There are two 'classic' foot infections ...

ATHLETE'S FOOT

This is a fungal growth between the toes. It is found in places that are warm and moist. It causes the skin to crack and peel, making it ITCHY.

- Keep feet CLEAN and DRY.
- Make sure you DRY IN BETWEEN YOUR TOES after showering.
- Use ATHLETE'S FOOT CREAM, SPRAY or TALCUM POWDER, available from the chemist.

VERRUCAS

These are warts on the feet and are easily spread. They are also hard to get rid of and can be painful. They are caused by a virus.

- Use a VERRUCA SOCK to prevent other people becoming infected.
- Apply OINTMENT to the affected area, available from the chemist.
- In severe cases, a DOCTOR OR CHIROPODIST will FREEZE DRY the VERRUCA off your foot.

AVOID IN THE FIRST PLACE BY USING FLIP-FLOPS IN COMMUNAL AREAS!

Tight Shoes

These cause three 'classic' problems ...

CORNS ... these are callouses of thick horny skin that form on joints of toes or balls of feet, where the foot has pressed hard against the shoe.

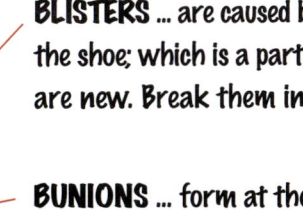

BLISTERS ... are caused by the foot rubbing against the shoe; which is a particular problem when shoes are new. Break them in carefully.

BUNIONS ... form at the joint between the big toe and the foot when the joint capsule becomes inflamed as a result of pressure from tight shoes.

POSTURE

Aspects Of Sport — 5

Good Posture Means ...

- All parts of the body are well ALIGNED.
- The LEAST STRAIN on muscles, tendons, ligaments and bones at joints.
- Being able to HOLD the body in the correct manner when STILL or MOVING.
- Maintenance of good muscle tone.
- Enabling major internal organs e.g. lungs to function efficiently.
- LOOKING GOOD!!!

Good Posture Is Achieved By ...

- Flexibility exercises for SUPPLENESS.
- Strength exercises for MUSCLE TONE.
- Standing, sitting, moving correctly i.e. with a STRAIGHT BACK.
- LIFTING and CARRYING objects correctly.

Poor Posture Means ...

- Part(s) of the body are out of ALIGNMENT.
- MORE STRAIN on and around joints, leading to pain and injury.
- Restricted space for internal organs to function efficiently.
- Muscular Weakness.
- LOOKING SLOPPY!!!

Poor Posture Can Be Caused By ...

- Uneven muscle development.
- Incorrect or over-exercise of a muscle.
- Standing, sitting, moving incorrectly.
- Incorrect lifting and carrying.
- Lack of balanced exercise.
- Bone or joint defects.
- Tiredness, inappropriate clothing, poor nutrition can also contribute.

Postural Defects Include

- Abnormal curvature of the spine ⟶ Strained back/abdominal muscles ⟶ permanent deformity.
- Rounded shoulders ⟶ restricted ability to breathe deeply.
- Uneven tilting of the hips ⟶ more strain on one leg, pressure on lower back muscles.

Lonsdale School Revision Guides

Safety Aspects 1 – DR ABC PROCEDURE

The help given to a casualty before the arrival of proper medical assistance is called FIRST AID. A competent FIRST AIDER can save a life by carrying out some basic procedures.

If a person has fainted, collapsed or been knocked out and is in an UNCONSCIOUS STATE then a first aider should initially carry out the DR ABC procedure.

DR ABC Procedure

D — DANGER

Assess the situation. Make sure that neither you or the casualty are in a dangerous situation.

HEALTH WARNING
ALL FIRST AID PROCEDURES SHOULD ONLY BE CARRIED OUT BY A COMPETENT FIRST AIDER WHO HAS BEEN TRAINED BY A PROPER AUTHORITY e.g. ST. JOHN AMBULANCE.

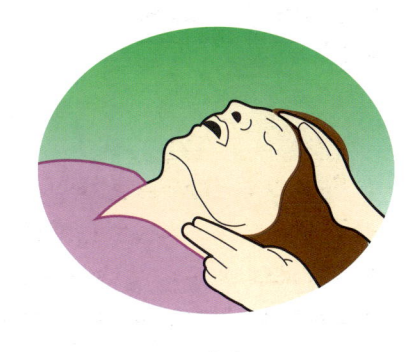

R — RESPONSE

Check for movement or speech and if there is none, send for help immediately. If there is a response, wait with the casualty until medical help arrives (but don't do anything to them).

A — AIRWAY

Check the airway is clear and open. If not, carefully use your fingers to remove any obstruction that may be blocking the airway, e.g. dirt, vomit, dentures, gum shield. Press the forehead backwards and the chin upwards.
This will move the tongue forward and away from the airway.
The airway should now be clear and fully open.

B — BREATHING

Check that the casualty is breathing. With the head back as described above...
- Listen carefully for the sound of breathing.
- Look to see if there is any upward and downward movement of the chest and abdomen.

If there is breathing, check for other injuries and await medical help.

C — CIRCULATION

The most reliable way of checking that the heart is circulating blood around the body is to feel the casualty's neck for a pulse. Place two fingers on the hollow between the trachea (wind pipe) and the neck muscle and press firmly. You should feel the carotid pulse.

What Happens Next

Make sure that PROPER MEDICAL ASSISTANCE is on its way. If you can't do this yourself get someone else to do it. If the casualty is breathing and has a pulse then the casualty should be placed in the RECOVERY POSITION and kept dry and warm until proper medical assistance arrives.

If the casualty is placed in the recovery position.
... the AIRWAY WILL REMAIN OPEN
... the TONGUE WILL ALWAYS BE IN A FORWARD POSITION
... any VOMIT WILL SEEP OUT of the mouth
... the LEGS AND ARMS PROVIDE STABILITY.

However ...
If the casualty is NOT BREATHING or HAS NO PULSE then the first aider needs to carry out MOUTH TO MOUTH RESUSCITATION (RESCUE BREATHING) and possibly CARDIAC MASSAGE until the arrival of proper medical assistance.

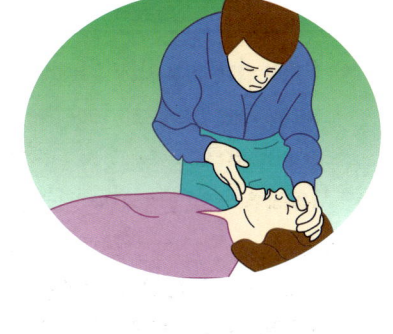

Safety Aspects 2 – MOUTH TO MOUTH RESUSCITATION

Mouth To Mouth Resuscitation (Rescue Breathing)

Mouth to mouth resuscitation should be carried out if the casualty has STOPPED BREATHING but STILL HAS A PULSE.

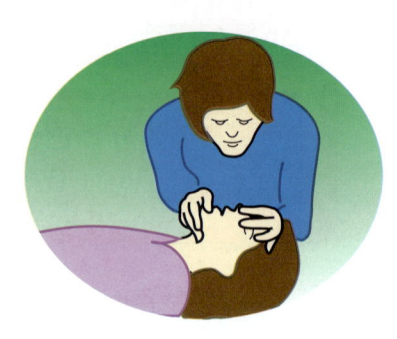

- Open the casualty's mouth wide and squeeze together the nostrils.
- Take a deep breath.

- Put your lips around the casualty's lips and breathe out into the mouth.
- Use a face shield or mask if available, it is more hygienic.
- You should notice the chest rise.

- Lift your mouth away.
- You should notice the chest fall.
- Take in another deep breath and repeat the process 12 times in one minute for an adult and 15 times in one minute for a child.
- Check for a pulse.

What Happens Next

There are three possibilities.

❶ The casualty STARTS TO BREATHE ON THEIR OWN without the need for mouth to mouth resuscitation and they STILL HAVE A PULSE.
Place in the RECOVERY POSITION until PROPER MEDICAL ASSISTANCE ARRIVES.

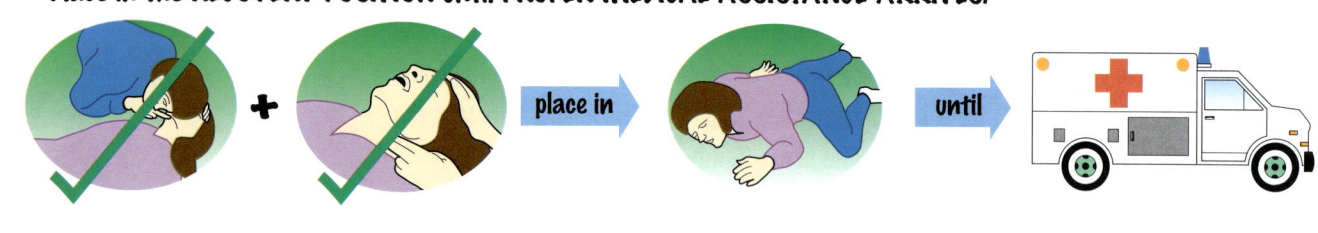

❷ The casualty DOES NOT START TO BREATHE ON THEIR OWN and they STILL HAVE A PULSE.
Carry on with MOUTH TO MOUTH RESUSCITATION until PROPER MEDICAL ASSISTANCE ARRIVES.

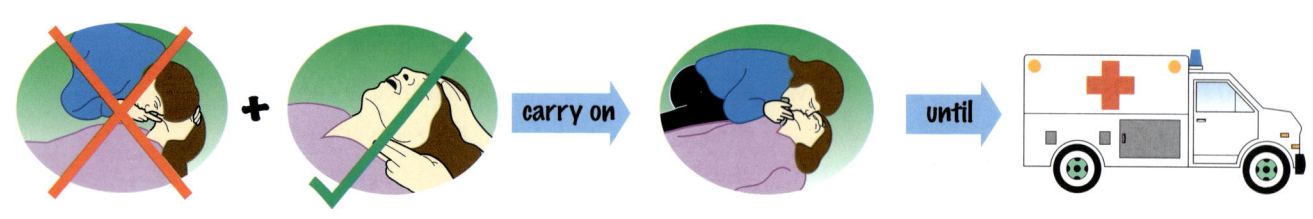

❸ The casualty DOES NOT START TO BREATHE ON THEIR OWN and they NOW HAVE NO PULSE.
The first aider now needs to carry out CARDIAC MASSAGE and MOUTH TO MOUTH RESUSCITATION until the arrival of PROPER MEDICAL ASSISTANCE.

Safety Aspects 3 – CARDIAC MASSAGE

Cardiac Massage

Cardiac massage should be carried out if the casualty's heart has **STOPPED BEATING** resulting in **NO PULSE BEING FELT.** It must be carried out alternately with mouth to mouth resuscitation.

- Locate the massage point. This is just above the meeting point of the breastbone and the rib junction.
- Place the heel of one hand, with the other hand on top, on the massage point.

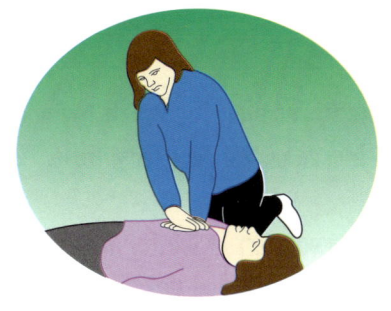

- With your arms straight press down on the breastbone until it depresses by 4 to 6cm for an adult and 2.5 to 4cm for a child.*
- Release the pressure.
- Complete 30 compressions, at a rate of 100 per minute

*If the casualty is a child, give 5 rescue breaths before beginning compressions.

- Complete 2 rescue breaths.
- Carry on by alternating between compressions and rescue breaths at the rate of 30 compressions followed by 2 breaths.

What Happens Next

Again there are three possibilities.

1 The casualty **STARTS TO BREATHE ON THEIR OWN** and a **PULSE CAN BE FELT.**
Place in the RECOVERY POSITION until PROPER MEDICAL ASSISTANCE ARRIVES.

2 The casualty **DOES NOT START TO BREATHE ON THEIR OWN** BUT a **PULSE CAN BE FELT.**
Carry on with MOUTH TO MOUTH RESUSCITATION until …
… the CASUALTY STARTS TO BREATHE ON THEIR OWN or PROPER MEDICAL ASSISTANCE ARRIVES.

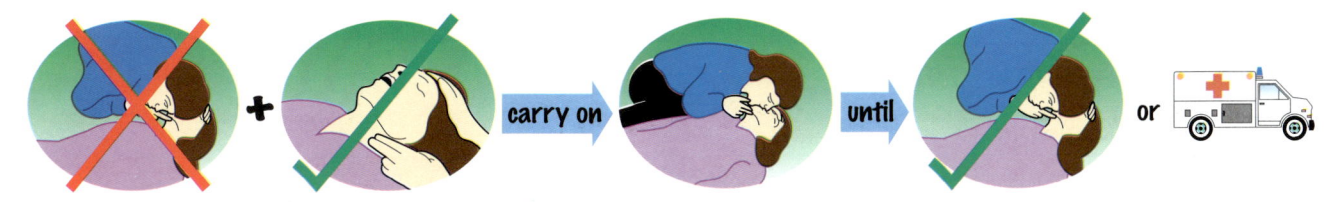

3 The casualty **DOES NOT START TO BREATHE ON THEIR OWN** and a **PULSE CANNOT BE FELT.**
Carry on with MOUTH TO MOUTH RESUSCITATION and CARDIAC MASSAGE until PROPER MEDICAL ASSISTANCE ARRIVES.

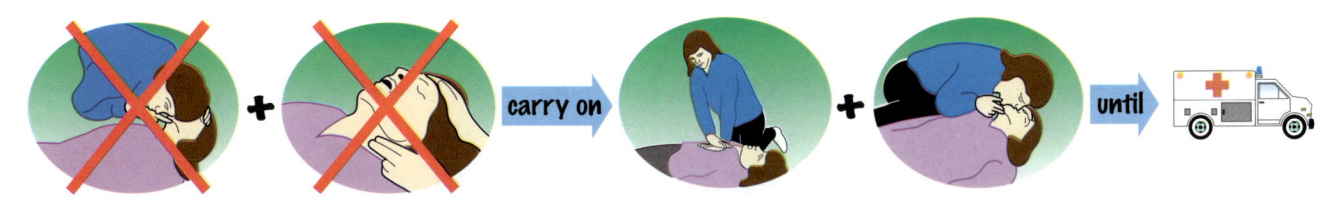

Safety Aspects 4 – R.I.C.E. TREATMENT

Aspects Of Sport 9

Sporting activity can put great demands on the body. At times the body is unable to cope and injury results. Some injuries require hospital treatment.
Many injuries however are minor and REST, ICE, COMPRESSION and ELEVATION or R.I.C.E. can be used to ease the pain and tenderness and shorten the time needed to recover.

R.I.C.E. Treatment

R ... for REST Allow the injury time to recover. Too much too soon ...
... will cause further damage and increase the recovery time.

I ... for ICE Cover the injured part in ice for 10 to 20 minutes. The coldness results ...
... in less blood flowing to the injured part reducing internal bleeding and swelling.

C ... for COMPRESSION Wrap a bandage not too tightly ...
around the injured part to provide support and immobilisation.
This will prevent further damage and reduce the swelling.

E ... for ELEVATION Raise the injured part.
Gravity reduces the amount of fluid collecting in the injured tissue ...
... and also the flow of blood into it.
This will reduce the swelling.

Suitable Injuries For R.I.C.E. Treatment

SPRAINS
Injuries to ligaments by wrenching or ...
... tearing around a joint ...
... are called SPRAINS.
They often occur through an ...
... ABRUPT TWISTING MOVEMENT ...
... at the joint.
The area involved will be SWOLLEN, SORE and BRUISED.

If you suspect the sprain is more damaging than you first thought, treat as a fracture and seek proper medical assistance.

STRAINS
Injuries where a muscle or tendon are ...
... overstretched or pulled with possible tearing ...
... are called STRAINS.
The area involved will be SWOLLEN and SORE ...
... with possibly ACUTE PAIN and
LOSS OF MOVEMENT.

If you suspect the strain is more damaging than you first thought, again seek proper medical assistance.

BRUISING
Most bruises can be treated with ICE ONLY to reduce the swelling and internal bleeding.
However ...
If the bruise is more serious then the R.I.C.E. procedure should be carried out.

Safety Aspects 5 – INJURIES REQUIRING HOSPITAL TREATMENT

Concussion

Concussion can arise after a person has suffered a head injury. It can lead to loss of memory, dizziness or even unconsciousness.

What You Should Do

- Make sure that PROPER MEDICAL ASSISTANCE is on its way.
- Carry out the DR ABC procedure (see page 45) ...
- If the casualty becomes unconscious take the relevant action (see pages 45, 46 and 47).

Fractures

A cracked or broken bone is called a fracture. During the breakage the casualty may well hear a crack. The area involved may show signs of swelling, bruising and deformity.

What You Should Do

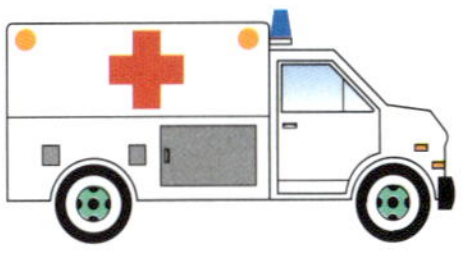

- Make sure that proper medical assistance is on its way.
- Do not attempt to move the casualty.
- If possible immobilise and give support to the injured site, e.g. putting a fractured arm in a sling or, if it is in the lower leg, fastening the two legs together.
- Your aim is to prevent movement to the injured site as this could cause further damage and discomfort.
- Try to keep the casualty warm and dry.
- Do not allow the casualty to eat or drink as this could delay the appropriate medical treatment.

Dislocations

The dislodging of a bone or bones at a joint is called a dislocation. The area involved may be swollen and bruised and appear twisted. The casualty may suffer severe pain and a lack of movement at the damaged joint.

What You Should Do

- Make sure that proper medical assistance is on its way.
- Do not attempt to move the casualty.
- If possible immobilise and give support to the injured joint.
- Your aim is to prevent movement of the injured joint as this could cause further damage.
- Do not apply pressure on the dislocated area.
- Do not attempt to put joints back in their proper position.
- Try to keep the casualty warm and dry.
- Do not allow the casualty to eat or drink as this could delay the appropriate medical treatment.

Torn Knee Cartilage

Knee cartilages can be torn or injured by a knock on the side of the knee or a sharp rotational movement at the joint. The area involved will be swollen and will be very painful, with the possibility that the knee may lock.

What You Should Do

- Make sure that proper medical assistance is on its way.
- Your aim is to prevent movement at the injury site.
- Try to keep the casualty warm and dry.
- Do not allow the casualty to eat or drink as this could delay the appropriate medical treatment.

Safety Aspects 6 – OTHER INJURIES AND AILMENTS

STITCH
Piercing pain in the side region of the body. Most likely to occur during exercise.

CRAMP
Extremely painful muscle seizure. Most likely to occur if you are tired, have been sweating a lot or after vigorous exercise.

SHOCK
Shock occurs when blood flow around the body is reduced. Can be caused by blood or fluid loss from the body. The skin will look pale, with the pulse getting weaker, followed by erratic behaviour and possibly unconsciousness.

CUTS AND GRAZES
A cut is the breaking of the skin with the release of blood from damaged blood vessels. A graze is the scraping of the skin. Both can occur during physical contact.

DEHYDRATION
Loss of water from the body. Most likely to occur during prolonged exercise with the person feeling limp and light-headed.

HYPOTHERMIA
Occurs when the body temperature is lowered to 35°C or below resulting in shivering. The skin will look pale with a slow pulse. Behaviour may become erratic. Can be caused by being outdoors for too long in the cold and wet. You should wrap casualty in warm clothing and shelter from wind and rain.

HEAT EXHAUSTION
Occurs when the body temp. is raised to 39°C or above resulting in erratic behaviour. The skin will look pale with a weak pulse. Can be caused by activity in hot, humid conditions when the body can't lose heat fast enough.

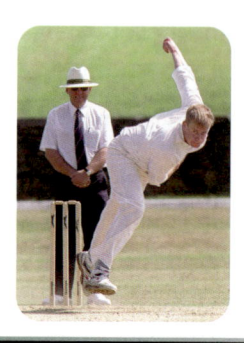

HEAT STROKE
Occurs when the body temp. is raised to extreme levels resulting in erratic behaviour. The skin will look hot with a bold pulse. Can be caused by activity in hot, humid conditions or it may follow heat exhaustion.

Factors Affecting Performance 1 – INTRODUCTION

Aspects Of Sport — 12

The factors can be broadly divided into three main categories ...

Psychological Factors

- Tension
- Anxiety/stress
- Motivation
- Personality
- Aggression
- Attitude

Physiological Factors

- Age
- Gender
- Body type
- Skill level
- Illness
- Injury
- Fatigue
- Diet
- Disability
- Lifestyle
- Body chemistry
- Drugs
- Blood doping

Environmental Factors

- Altitude
- Humidity
- Pollution
- Weather
- Large crowd

Many of these factors are discussed in greater detail on the following pages ...
... or in other sections of the book.

Lonsdale School Revision Guides

Factors Affecting Performance 2 – ENVIRONMENT, PRESSURE, DISABILITY, ILLNESS
Aspects Of Sport — 13

Environment

Altitude
The atmosphere is thinner ...
- Less OXYGEN available
- Endurance reduced
- Risk of dehydration

'Thin' air may enhance power/anaerobic events: less 'air resistance' eg. Javelin, Long Jump

Pollution
Can affect ...
- The Respiratory System: uptake of O_2
- The lungs could be irritated by pollutants
- Aerobic/endurance events more difficult

Weather
Wind, rain, sun, heat, cold can affect ...
- Technique: skill production
- Tactics: short passing in windy conditions

Humidity
Can affect ...
- Temperature regulation (See p37)
- Dehydration (See p37)

Pressure/Stress

Individual
- Alone, no support
- No-one to blame

With a partner
- Will I let him down?
- Will he let me down?

Part of a team
- Do I deserve my place?
- Am I doing my job?
- Will I get the blame?

In front of a crowd
- Will I embarrass myself?
- Too nervous?

Quality of opposition
- Opponent too good, anxiety, tension
- Not good enough, complacent, over-confident

Level of competition
- Loss of confidence
- Loss of interest

Physical Disability

- May be unable to perform skills in the conventional way. Adapt technique.
- Rules may be modified in order for participation.
- Other abilities may compensate eg. wheelchair athletes - upper body strength.

"I am an athlete with a disability, not a disabled athlete."
Tanni Grey-Thompson

Illness/Fatigue

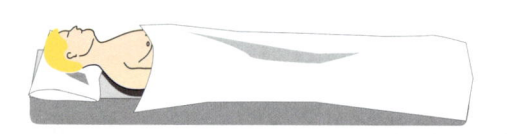

- More likely to make errors.
- Poor levels of concentration.
- Unlikely to perform at one's best!

Factors Affecting Performance 3 – SOMATOTYPE

Aspects Of Sport — 14

Body Shape

Body shape is described by SOMATOTYPING. A SOMATOTYPE uses a 'triangular' graph with 3 axes ranging from 1 to 7 to describe how a person's physique relates to three extremes.

These extremes are ENDOMORPH (fat), MESOMORPH (muscular) and ECTOMORPH (thin). The values for somatotype are always stated in this order. Thus an extreme ectomorph is 117 whilst an extreme endomorph is 711.

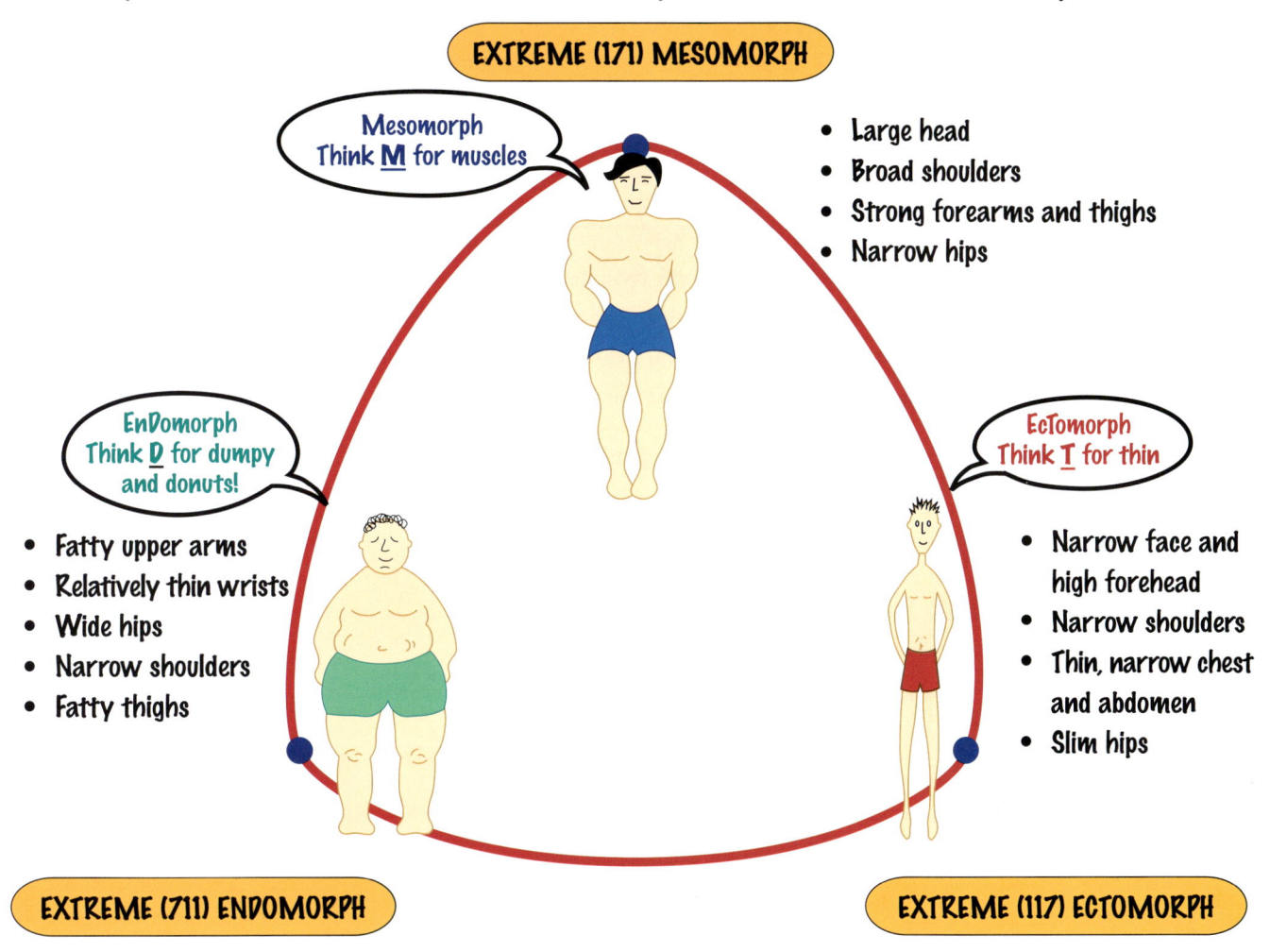

EXTREME (171) MESOMORPH

Mesomorph — Think **M** for muscles

- Large head
- Broad shoulders
- Strong forearms and thighs
- Narrow hips

EnDomorph — Think **D** for dumpy and donuts!

- Fatty upper arms
- Relatively thin wrists
- Wide hips
- Narrow shoulders
- Fatty thighs

EcTomorph — Think **T** for thin

- Narrow face and high forehead
- Narrow shoulders
- Thin, narrow chest and abdomen
- Slim hips

EXTREME (711) ENDOMORPH

EXTREME (117) ECTOMORPH

Somatotypes Of Performers

All people are a mixture of different proportions of all three types, with characteristics from each extreme. Sports people, however, tend to have strong Mesomorphic characteristics, since muscle plays such a large part in most sports.

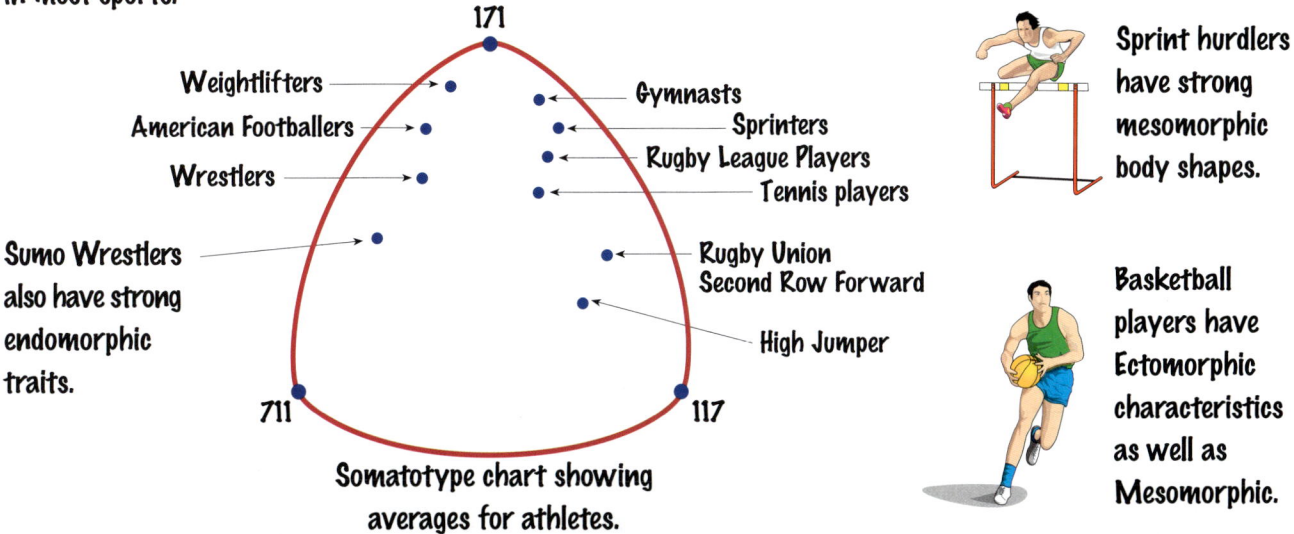

Somatotype chart showing averages for athletes.

- 171 (top)
- Weightlifters
- American Footballers
- Wrestlers
- Gymnasts
- Sprinters
- Rugby League Players
- Tennis players
- Sumo Wrestlers also have strong endomorphic traits.
- Rugby Union Second Row Forward
- High Jumper
- 711 (bottom left)
- 117 (bottom right)

Sprint hurdlers have strong mesomorphic body shapes.

Basketball players have Ectomorphic characteristics as well as Mesomorphic.

Factors Affecting Performance 4 – GENDER, AGE, LIFESTYLE

Aspects Of Sport — 15

Gender

After the first eleven years of your life, being a boy or a girl makes a difference in shaping your sporting potential. There are 6 main differences to remember (N.B. These are generalisations)...

Strength — Males have more muscle than females. On average males are 50% stronger. The male hormone testosterone encourages the growth of bone and muscle.

Cardiovascular Endurance — Males have larger hearts and lungs, and more blood.

Bone Structure — Males tend to have bigger bones which makes them larger and heavier than females. The Female pelvis is wider than the males, for childbirth. The male's more narrow pelvis allows power to be transmitted to the lower body more effectively.

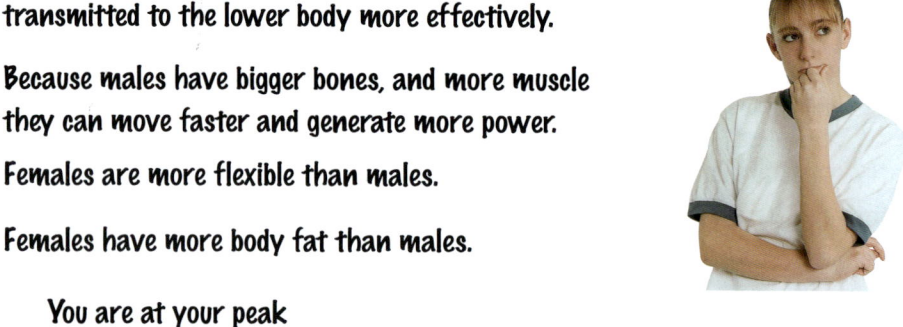

Speed and Power — Because males have bigger bones, and more muscle they can move faster and generate more power.

Flexibility — Females are more flexible than males.

Body fat — Females have more body fat than males.

Age

You are at your peak fitness in your 20's.

FORMATIVE YEARS (CHILDHOOD) — Skill levels develop through variety of experiences, and the ingraining of 'good habits' e.g. regular practice.

"Fitness"

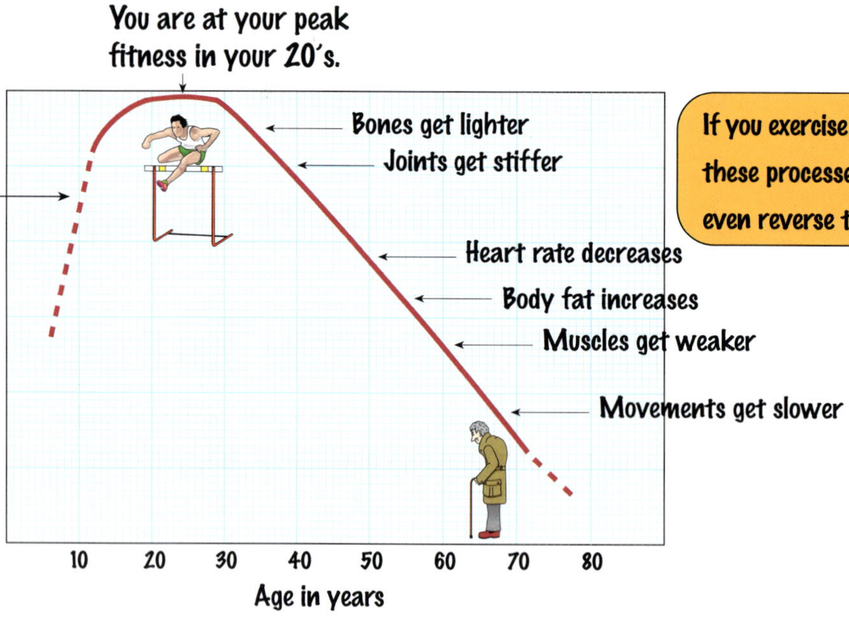

- Bones get lighter
- Joints get stiffer
- Heart rate decreases
- Body fat increases
- Muscles get weaker
- Movements get slower

If you exercise you can slow these processes down and even reverse them.

Age in years: 10 20 30 40 50 60 70 80

Lifestyle

The way you choose to live your life can have serious implications for your performance on the sports field.

- Call for a drink on the way home and maybe get a curry. 
- Out clubbing tonight with the boys! 
- Good lie in on Sunday morning.  
- Extra training this afternoon. Practice my heading? 
- mmm... nice night in tonight with a good book, then early to bed. 
- Weight training on Sunday morning!

Factors Affecting Performance 5 – PERSONALITY AND MINDSET

Personality Of The Performer

Personality is a very complicated subject and there are an infinite number of possible personalities. However, broadly speaking, we can sub-divide people into EXTROVERTS and INTROVERTS.

EXTROVERTS tend to be ...
... chatty, animated, outgoing 'risk takers,' who prefer contact sports and team games involving plenty of action and drama.

INTROVERTS tend to be ...
... shy, deliberate, quiet 'risk assessors,' who prefer non-contact sports and individual games involving strategical thinking and tactics.

It's important to remember that these are just generalisations.

Getting The Mind-set Right

ANXIETY ... is often caused by fear of UNDER-PERFORMING, particularly if the stakes are high or the crowd is large.

MOTIVATION ... is your real reason for striving so hard. It could be because you want to be the best at your sport or you just might want to make money. It's difficult to succeed without real motivation.

Football Managers experience a full range of emotions!

TENSION ... due to anxiety, causes over-production of adrenaline and possibly nausea together with light-headedness. Actual physical tension can reduce effectiveness of muscles.

ADRENALINE ... is produced by getting psyched-up for your event. It causes increased heart rate, diversion of blood to your muscles and increased breathing ready for 'fight or flight.'

Aggression

Aggression is defined as behaving in a way that is intended to cause harm to someone else. The aggression is said to be channelled if it is used in order to achieve a goal. It may take two forms ...

DIRECT AGGRESSION
Towards an opponent's body
e.g. Rugby, Boxing, Wrestling.

INDIRECT AGGRESSION
Channelled through an object (a ball) towards your opponent
e.g. Tennis, Cricket.

Factors Affecting Performance 6 – SUBSTANCE ABUSE

An A - Z Of Artificial Aids

Alcohol
, can induce feelings of well-being and lack of responsibility. It is a form of 'escape.' Unfortunately it can lead to aggression, reduced muscle glycogen, kidney and liver damage and lack of motivation.

Anabolic Agents
(steroids). These accelerate the growth and repair of muscle, and so are abused to help athletes "bulk-up" for explosive events. This can cause heart and blood pressure problems, excess aggression, male characteristics in females and loss of fertility.

Beta Blockers
These are taken by performers to help them to relax because they counteract the effect of adrenaline. Used particularly in snooker and darts. Can cause low blood pressure, insomnia, depression and lack of mental 'edge.'

Blood Doping
. After training at altitude an athlete can remove haemoglobin-rich blood from his body and freeze it prior to re-injection before a competition. The main danger is increased blood density and blockage.

Diuretics
, increase water loss from the body by urination. In boxing, judo, wrestling and weightlifting, competition is limited by weight category and therefore quick weight loss can be important, but sodium and potassium is lost as well.

Peptide Hormones, Mimetics and Analogues,
can increase the production of muscle in a similar way to steroids. They can also be used to increase the production of red blood cells to improve oxygen transport. They can cause infertility and blood pressure problems. Most common types are Erythropoietin (EPO) and Human Growth Hormone (h.G.H).

Narcotic Analgesics
(pain killers). These are used to suppress pain from athletic injuries so that the performer can still compete. Heroin, morphine and codeine are three examples. Invasive pain can lead to worsening of the original injury.

Stimulants
, make people feel "high" and "up for it." They increase the activity of the cardiovascular system and the central nervous system. After use, a person may feel depressed and listless. Blood pressure may become high.

Tobacco
, apparently can help people to relax but the price you have to pay is increased heart rate and blood pressure, lowered O_2 carrying capacity, blocked coronary arteries, increased risk of cancer, smokers cough, emphysema, bronchitis etc etc.

Factors Affecting Performance 7 – ACQUISITION OF SKILL

Skill

"Skill is acquired ability to bring about a desired result as efficiently as possible with confidence in the eventual outcome." It is learning to do a specific thing with accuracy and efficiency. You know what to do and so you do it, exactly how you want to without wasting any more of your time than necessary. This is being skilful.

OPEN ← There are two types of skill → **CLOSED**

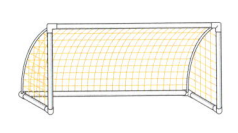

What you do to achieve the same outcome may vary. A Goalkeeper's skill is open. He has to stop the ball from going in the net. The way he does this depends on how the ball is aimed.

You do the same thing over and over again, in exactly the same way. A golfer's skill is closed. The skill is repeated in the same way.

There are 4 ways in which you can practice

Whole Practice 
This is where you repeat the whole exercise over and over again. For example in an activity which doesn't lend itself to being split into parts, like dribbling a football.

Variable Practice
This type of practice is important when learning open skill. It is where you practice the skill in lots of different settings. For example a cricketer plays his shots according to the type and speed of delivery he receives.

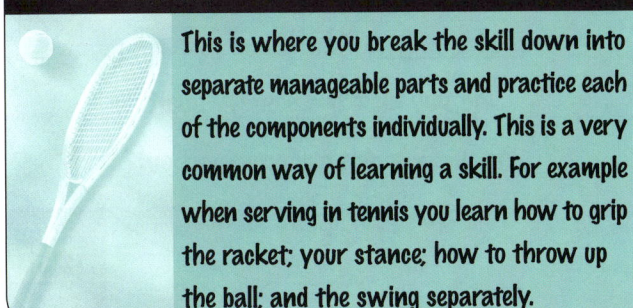

Part Practice
This is where you break the skill down into separate manageable parts and practice each of the components individually. This is a very common way of learning a skill. For example when serving in tennis you learn how to grip the racket; your stance; how to throw up the ball; and the swing separately.

Fixed Practice 
This type of practice is used for learning a closed skill. A skill is repeated under the same environmental conditions. For example a golfer will practice his long iron or driver shots repeatedly. The setting of the skill doesn't change.

Guidance

Guidance is the help you can receive when learning a new skill

VISUAL – WHAT YOU SEE
You learn how to perform a skill by watching first. This may be a one to one demonstration or you could watch a video or look at a series of pictures. This could give a clear image in the performer's mind of what's required.

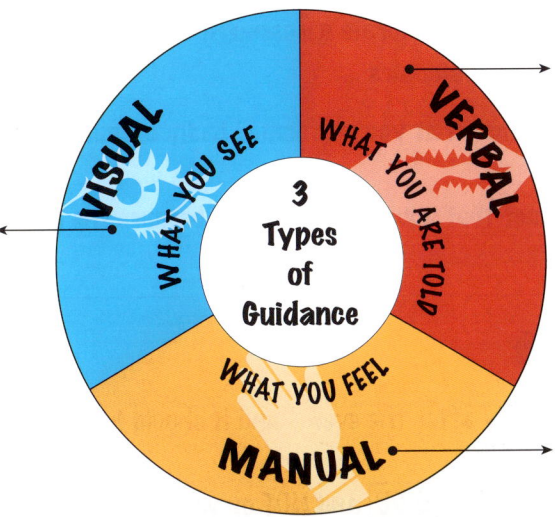

VERBAL – WHAT YOU ARE TOLD
A skill may be explained using words, either by your coach or teacher. The explanation could be used to highlight the most important parts of the visual guidance.

MANUAL – WHAT YOU FEEL
You are physically guided or manhandled through the motions of a new skill in order to learn it. You get a feel for what you should be doing. Your muscles can experience what the movement should feel like. This creates MUSCLE MEMORY.

3 Types of Guidance

Factors Affecting Performance 8 – FEEDBACK

Aspects Of Sport — 19

The Feedback Loop

Without feedback you are performing in a 'vacuum.' Feedback allows you to assess your performance and use this assessment to inform your next performance ...

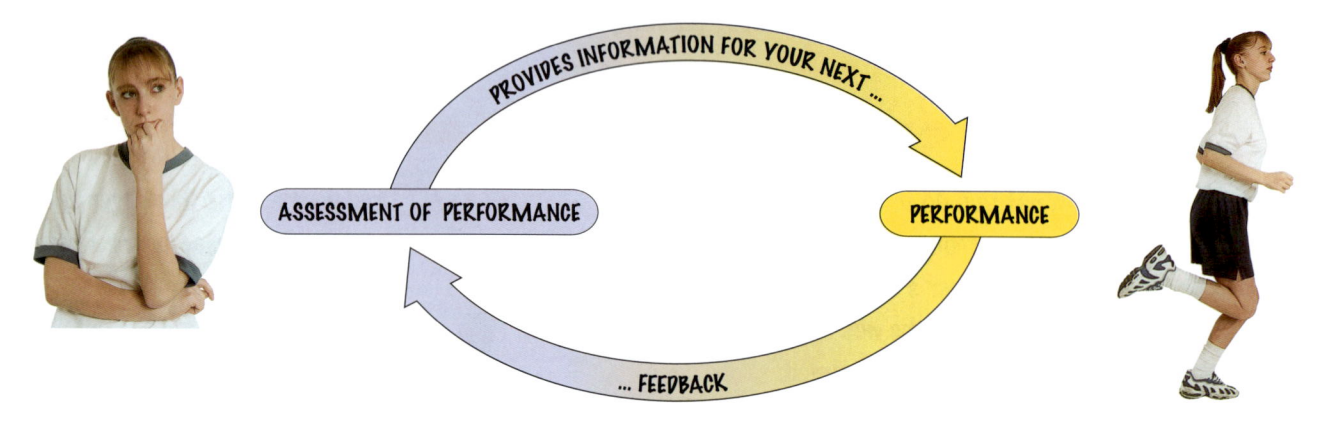

PROVIDES INFORMATION FOR YOUR NEXT ...
ASSESSMENT OF PERFORMANCE → PERFORMANCE
... FEEDBACK

The Components Of Feedback

There are just two components of feedback ...
... KP and KR ...

KNOWLEDGE OF PERFORMANCE ...
... tells you how you performed <u>irrespective of the results</u> and comes from your coach, fellow players, spectators or even video evidence. Not least, you yourself can sense how you did.

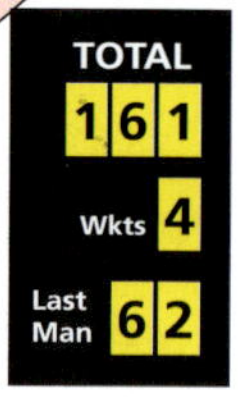

+

KNOWLEDGE OF RESULTS ...
... tells you whether you achieved your particular result <u>irrespective of your performance</u>. Did the ball go for 4? Did you kick the penalty goal? Did you knock your opponent out? Was your serve an ace?

TOTAL 161
Wkts 4
Last Man 62

ASSESSMENT OF PERFORMANCE

Correct use of KP and KR will give you an accurate assessment of how you performed and will avoid the possibility of two 'false' outcomes ...

A) You won but this 'disguises' the fact that you performed badly because the opposition were weak or you fluked it.

B) You lost and this 'masks' the fact that you performed well because the opposition were strong or they fluked it.

Using Feedback Effectively

- Feedback should be **FAST** (immediately after the event) and it should be **FOCUSED** (on the key areas for concern), and you need to think about it.
- It should concentrate on **WHAT YOU NEED TO DO** and NOT on what you did wrong. Feedback should be positive.

TECHNOLOGY IN SPORT

Aspects Of Sport — 20

Effect Of Technology

Technological developments have had an impact on EQUIPMENT and MATERIALS used in sport. This has had an effect on PARTICIPATION and PERFORMANCE in different activities and for different performers.

Equipment
Use of GRAPHITE or a manmade material such as CARBON TITANIUM FIBRE to make Tennis Rackets or Golf Clubs lighter and more powerful.

Clothing and Footwear
Clothes have become lightweight, breathable, aerodynamic and more comfortable, keeping the participant cool, dry and able to perform better. Grip fins on some football boots enable the ball to swerve more.

NEW TECHNOLOGY

ICT Information Communication Technology
Records data for analysis of performance. Pressure Sensitive Blocks in Athletics are linked to a timing system and this helps to avoid a sprinter "jumping the gun." Electronic Net Sensors calculate the percentage of first serves in Tennis that are accurate.

Digital Cameras and Video
Cameras provide an accurate knowledge of performance whose analysis is a component of FEEDBACK. Filming all aspects of the game provides a fuller picture of the individual's or team's performance. Used in a whole range of different sports e.g. Football, Rugby, Athletics and with the advent of underwater cameras, swimming and diving.

An example which combines a number of new technologies is a 100m sprint.

- The race can be timed accurately to within 100ths of a second, using ICT.
- Athletes wear aerodynamic clothing and specific footwear.
- An exact and measurable picture taken with a camera aids the decision-making process of which athlete came where.

New Technology And Training Aids

Heart Rate Monitors
Often in the form of a wrist watch, they can provide exact measurements of HEART RATE. This informs the athlete of training intensity.

Power Analysis
Currently used by cyclists, there are sensors on the pedals which inform cyclists of how much power is being applied to the pedals. This is likely to be available in running shoes in the future.

SPONSORSHIP 1

Issues In Sport — 1

What It Is And How It Works

Sponsorship is the provision of **FINANCIAL** or **MATERIAL ASSISTANCE** by a third party, e.g. a business. In return it receives **PUBLICITY** through its association with the sport, the club or the performer.

MONEY/EQUIPMENT/COACHING/FACILITIES/TRAVEL/FOOD →

ASSISTANCE IN EXCHANGE FOR PUBLICITY

← ADVERTISING/MEDIA COVERAGE/LOGO/GOOD IMAGE

RECIPIENTS OF SPONSORSHIP

- A **SPORT** ...
  ... e.g. Amateur Swimming Association
- A **TEAM** ...
  ... e.g. any Premiership football team
- An **EVENT** ...
  ... e.g. World Snooker Championship
- A **COMPETITION** ...
  ... e.g. the Super League (Rugby League)
- An **INDIVIDUAL** ...
  ... personal contracts with sportswear companies

TYPES OF SPONSORSHIP

- **MONEY** ...
  ... for living expenses
- **KIT AND EQUIPMENT** ...
  ... e.g. sportswear, tennis racquets etc
- **TRAVEL** ...
  ... e.g. a car
- **SCHOLARSHIPS** ...
  ... to attend a Centre of Excellence
- **FOOD** ...
  ... to help with sport-specific diets

MANY OTHER EXAMPLES OF SPONSORSHIP CAN BE FOUND BOTH NATIONALLY AND LOCALLY.

Negative Effects Of Sponsorship

In return for their investment sponsors expect MAXIMUM MEDIA EXPOSURE. To achieve this they can influence:

THE DATE, TIME AND PLACE OF AN EVENT

In the 1994 FIFA WORLD CUP - USA matches scheduled to suit TV meant playing in dangerously high temperatures.

PERSONAL APPEARANCES AFTER AN EVENT

Recipients are expected to attend press conferences after an event, making sure the sponsor's logo is given maximum exposure.

RULE, LAW AND EVEN SEASON CHANGES

This is done to create greater audience appeal. Cricket now has 'limited over' matches under floodlights. Rugby League has changed to a summer sport in exchange for a huge investment from satellite TV.

SPONSORSHIP 2

Issues In Sport — 2

Obtaining Sponsorship

Major sports, individuals, teams and events which are popular and successful easily attract sponsorship. Minority sports, individuals, teams and events that may have less 'public interest' find sponsorship more difficult to attract because they appeal to a smaller audience.

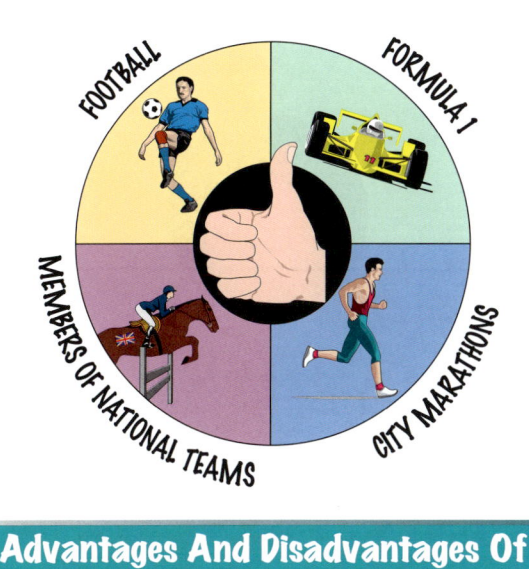

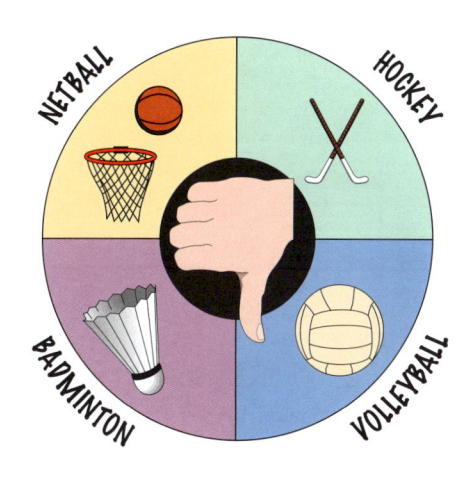

Thumbs up: FOOTBALL, FORMULA 1, MEMBERS OF NATIONAL TEAMS, CITY MARATHONS

Thumbs down: NETBALL, HOCKEY, BADMINTON, VOLLEYBALL

Advantages And Disadvantages Of Sponsorship

Sponsorship is intended to benefit both the recipient and the sponsor ...
... however there are advantages and disadvantages for both.

FOR THE SPORT, INDIVIDUAL, EVENT

ADVANTAGES
- AIDS DEVELOPMENT ... of young potential stars
- REDUCES FINANCIAL PRESSURES ...
  ... enabling training and competing to be full time.
- FUNDS EVENTS ...
  ... by covering the organisational and administrational costs.
- PROVISION ...
  ... of coaching, equipment, travel, specialist facilities.
- INCREASED INCOME ...
  ... resulting in superstar salary status.

DISADVANTAGES
- EXPLOITATION ...
  ... to suit the sponsor's needs.
- LENGTH OF CONTRACT ...
  ... may be short which provides less security.
- SUPPORT MAY BE WITHDRAWN ...
  ... if the sponsor's income becomes reduced.
- MINORITY SPORTS MAY DECLINE ...
  ... as major sports attract most sponsorship.
- WRONG IMAGE PRESENTED ...
  ... through tobacco, alcohol sponsorship.

FOR THE SPONSOR

ADVANTAGES
- SUCCESS, HEALTH, POPULARITY ...
  ... is associated with the sponsor
- MEDIA COVERAGE ...
  ... is a powerful advertising outlet
- LOGOS OR BRAND NAMES ...
  ... become well known and recognised
- OFTEN TAX DEDUCTIBLE ...
  ... can be set against profits to reduce tax

DISADVANTAGES
- RISK ELEMENT ...
  ... since success in sport is not guaranteed
- MEDIA COVERAGE ...
  ... may reduce or even cease
- WRONG IMAGE PRESENTED ...
  ... with hooliganism at events ...
  ... poor behaviour of individual or team sponsored.

Lonsdale School Revision Guides

THE MEDIA AND SPORT 1

Issues In Sport — 3

The Media

The MEDIA keeps us INFORMED, ENTERTAINED and ENLIGHTENED. Sport provides the media with NEWS, EVENTS and SENSATIONALISM which attracts public interest. The different forms of media are constantly growing and changing with advances in TECHNOLOGY and are completely unrecognisable from 50 years ago.

Types Of Media Coverage

Media coverage is controlled by the people who run it i.e. the MEDIA OWNERS, EDITORS, DIRECTORS, PRODUCERS, REPORTERS, CAMERA OPERATORS. They influence public opinion by the pictures they show and the articles they write.

MEDIA	AUDIENCE	TYPE OF COVERAGE
INTERNET	(1)	Fast information access. Possibly educational and/or entertaining.
VIDEO/FILM	(1)	Recorded entertainment (best action). Educational (coaching series).
BOOKS	(1)	Stories behind events, Biographies - for leisure or education.
MAGAZINES	(3)	Specialised or general - informative and educational.
RADIO	(4)	Informative and entertaining with results, reports, comments etc.
NEWSPAPERS (Tabloid and broadsheet)	(5)	Informative - results, reports, balanced views, opinions etc. Entertaining - sensational stories, private lives exposed. Educational - tips to develop skills, fitness.
TELEVISION (Terrestrial - licence fee. Satellite, Cable, Digital, Interactive - all subscription or pay per view)	(7)	Informative - results, reports, comment, text, live action, highlights. Entertaining - live action, highlights, specialised programmes. Educational - documentaries, coaching series, live action, highlights, specific programmes for schools.

THE MEDIA AND SPORT 2

Issues In Sport — 4

Effects Of Media Coverage

THE GOOD,

- Promotes and popularises traditional and new sports.
- Generates finance, e.g. sponsorship, which can be used for junior development.
- Informs, enlightens and instructs.
- Technological innovations have resulted in better coverage, analysis, statistics.
- Raising awareness and interest which results in greater participation.
- Creates feedback for participants, coaches, officials.
- Creates 'star performers' who may become positive role models.
- Ever increasing audiences (worldwide via TV) result in increasing sponsorship.

THE BAD

- Some sports will go into decline if they receive little media attention.
- Increases the pressure to succeed for participants, managers, coaches, officials.
- Over-exposure leading to audience boredom.
- Exaggerated and sensational stories to attract audiences or consumers.
- Live coverage of events can reduce potential attendance.
- Sports are forced to change schedules, dates, seasons to suit TV or sponsors.

AND THE UGLY

- Publicises the poor behaviour of some participants, spectators.
- Can create 'win at all cost' attitude, 'gamesmanship', cheating.
- Makes sport 'life-or-death' which intensifies rivalries between supporters.

In Summary

The MEDIA is BIG BUSINESS and is an ORGANISATION DRIVEN BY PROFIT. To do this it has STRONG LINKS with ADVERTISING and SPONSORSHIP.

SPORTS AUDIENCE → Attracts... → MEDIA ATTENTION, ADVERTISING, SPONSORSHIP → Which Results In... → MONEY GENERATED FOR SPORT

MEDIA ATTENTION, ADVERTISING, SPONSORSHIP → Which Results In... → MONEY GENERATED FOR THE MEDIA, ADVERTISERS AND SPONSORS

SPORTING BEHAVIOUR

Issues In Sport — **5**

Good Sporting Behaviour

Sport, ideally, provides both participants and spectators with an emotional outlet for the tensions created by everyday life. Good sporting behaviour should involve controlled aggression against an opponent (or object) within rules or regulations enforced by officials.

PARTICIPANTS *for...* ... *to produce...* **ENTERTAINMENT and DRAMA** *for...* **SPECTATORS** *who create...* **ATMOSPHERE, SUPPORT and POSITIVE ENCOURAGEMENT**

Good sporting behaviour also involves ETIQUETTE ...
... where a participant shows ...
... RESPECT, HONOUR and COURTESY ...
... for the OPPONENTS and the GAME.

If you should meet with TRIUMPH or DISASTER treat both IMPOSTERS just the same ...
— Rudyard Kipling

Examples are:
- Acknowledging opponent's good play.
- 'Walking' in cricket when out.
- Conceding a putt in golf.

Bad Sporting Behaviour

Bad sporting behaviour by a participant often leads to a spectator response. Spectators may react badly to ...

- Over-aggression i.e. foul play
- Professional foul with a deliberate infringement
- Officials not acting firmly and justly
- Players contesting the rules with officials
- Gamesmanship i.e. 'diving', time wasting
- Unfair tactics i.e. cheating
- Sledging and psyching out of opponent

It has often been assumed that CONTACT SPORTS result in VIOLENT BEHAVIOUR among spectators and NON-CONTACT SPORTS result in NON-VIOLENT BEHAVIOUR among spectators. This assumption as yet has not been proven!!

Football Hooliganism

For many years there was much debate and concern over crowd behaviour in and around football grounds. Two tragedies, Heysel in 1985 and Hillsborough in 1989, led to a GOVERNMENT ENQUIRY to prevent future tragedies and to combat crowd violence. The result was ...

... THE TAYLOR REPORT
Recommendations and other measures included:
- Removal of perimeter fences.
- Segregation of fans.
- All seater stadiums.
- CCTV.
- The sharing of 'intelligence' about trouble makers by different Police forces

AMATEUR AND PROFESSIONAL SPORT

Issues In Sport — 6

Amateurs, Semi-Professionals And Professionals

People compete in sport as either AMATEURS, SEMI-PROFESSIONALS or PROFESSIONALS. The status of a competitor for a particular sport is defined by set rules laid down by the Governing Body for that sport. In most cases amateurs and professionals do not compete together, although some sports e.g. golf, tennis are 'OPEN'.

A FEW PROFESSIONALS
Full time players expected to reach the highest standards.

SOME SEMI-PROFESSIONALS
They are part time players, committed to their sport, performing at a very good level.

MANY AMATEURS
Spare time players who provide most sport participants. It is possible for players to keep their amateur status and do their sport FULL TIME through …
- SCHOLARSHIP - athletes at specialist colleges
- TRUST FUND - use prize/appearance money to pay 'expenses'
- SPONSORSHIP - by a private enterprise } with the approval of
- GRANT - from Sports Aid } Sports Governing Body
- JOB/OCCUPATION - Generous employer allowing (much) time off to train and compete

These may be seen as 'loopholes', allowing amateurs to earn from their sport.

Traditional Differences Between Amateurs And Professionals

AMATEURS
- Receive no FINANCIAL REWARDS i.e. PAYMENTS.
- Play or compete for PLEASURE.
- Originally they were 'Gentlemen' from a HIGHER SOCIAL CLASS with the TIME and MONEY to play sport.

PROFESSIONALS
- Receive PAYMENT for PLAYING and COMPETING.
- Play or compete as a CAREER.
- Originally they were 'WORKING CLASS' men with sporting talent who were paid to compensate for time lost from work to play and compete.

Changing Face Of Athletics And Rugby

Commercial interest in a particular sport increases the amount of money available and the need for amateur status diminishes. Athletics and Rugby Union are two such sports.

ATHLETICS
- Olympics and World Class events present commercial opportunities.
- Competitors can receive financial assistance or reward, subject to certain rules … … e.g. no 'direct' payment
- Amateurism is a concept being phased out at elite level e.g. Grand Prix prizes.

RUGBY
- In 1895 rugby became two separate codes.

  AMATEUR UNION || 1895 || PROFESSIONAL LEAGUE

- Both attract commercial interest, but only rugby league openly rewards players.
- Increasing International pressure for rugby union to relax its amateur rules.
  In 1995 rugby union became a professional sport.

FACILITIES AND PROVIDERS

Issues In Sport — 7

Types Of Facility

- These either fall into one of two categories ...

1. PURPOSE BUILT
Single or multi-activity.
e.g. Leisure Centres and Clubs

2. NATURAL ENVIRONMENT
Hills, Lakes, Rivers Seaside etc.
e.g. National Parks

... or they may be a combination of both.

PURPOSE BUILT AROUND FEATURES OF NATURAL ENVIRONMENT
e.g. Artificial Ski Slopes, Water Sports Centres, Activity Holiday Centres.

- FACILITIES are built and located to provide a range of challenges. Outdoor education centres like PLAS Y BRENIN make the most of the advantages of the natural environment whilst at the same time maximising the challenges for the performer.

Providers Of Facilities

- They can either be LOCAL or NATIONAL.

LOCAL PROVIDERS

1. LOCAL AUTHORITIES, TOWN AND PARISH COUNCILS, VOLUNTARY CLUBS, COMMUNITY PARTNERSHIPS, REGIONAL SPORTS COUNCILS. These are run by committees who often employ sport development officers and are non-profit making.
2. PRIVATE ENTERPRISE inc. private clubs, gyms. The commercial leisure/fitness industry exists to look after its members and are profit making.
3. PRIVATE ENTERPRISE OPERATING AUTHORITY-OWNED FACILITIES. It is possible for private companies to run public facilities. They are profit making.

NATIONAL PROVIDERS

1. SPORT ENGLAND, SPORTS GOVERNING BODIES. These provide centres of excellence for elite athletes and developing talent.
2. VOLUNTARY ORGANISATIONS e.g. NATIONAL TRUST. These provide leisure pursuits and activities for the general public. They are often charities.
3. PRIVATE ENTERPRISE e.g. HOTELS, DAVID LLOYD CENTRES. These exist to cater for private members and to make a profit for shareholders, owners and franchise operations.

Factors Affecting The Location Of Facilities

- There are many but all you have to do is remember all these 'P's.

PUBLIC ACCESSIBILITY ... transport links.

PRICE ... cost to build, possible grants and lottery funds.

APPROPRIATE SURROUNDINGS.

LOCATION

PUBLIC NEEDS ... for families, elite athletes, minority groups.

PLANNING AUTHORISATION ... may depend on environmental impact.

POPULATION ... i.e. paying public.

HOW A SPORTS CLUB WORKS

Issues In Sport — 8

How A Sports Club Works

A sports club exists ...
... for its members to enjoy participation in `PLAYING`, `SOCIAL` and `ADMINISTRATION ACTIVITIES`.
In return for an annual membership fee or subscription the club should provide:

- `FACILITIES` - for playing and changing.
- `FIXTURES/COMPETITIONS/TOURNAMENTS`.
- `COACHING` - progressing from 'beginner level' to 'representative level.'

These provisions are organised and run by a `COMMITTEE OF ELECTED MEMBERS`.
A typical committee may consist of ...

CHAIR PERSON
Highest official who has a controlling vote.

MEMBERSHIP SECRETARY
Keeps records of all members and their status.

FIXTURES SECRETARY
Arranges matches and venues for all the teams.

A calendar of regular meetings will discuss an AGENDA which may include:
- FINANCIAL POSITION
- MAINTENANCE
- ACTIVITIES
- DEVELOPMENT AND PLANNING
- ANY OTHER ISSUES RAISED BY MEMBERS

CLUB SECRETARY
Records meetings, distributes information to members.

TREASURER
Manages financial records. Produces current 'balance sheet' showing PROFIT or LOSS.

- ... while `SUB-COMMITTEES` have the following responsibilities.

  - SELECTION
  - TOURNAMENTS
  - FUND RAISING
  - COACHING
  - SOCIAL EVENTS
  - JUNIORS

Outside Links With Schools And Communities

Sport's National and Regional Governing Bodies and Local Authorities encourage sports clubs to forge links with SCHOOLS and COMMUNITIES to increase the opportunities for `PARTICIPATION` and `DEVELOPMENT OF TALENT`. They do this by providing:

- **FUNDING GRANTS** - to improve facilities.
- **DEVELOPMENT OFFICERS** - who run 'awareness' schemes to attract raw talent and new members.
- **SHARED USE OF FACILITIES** - school pitches, courts, gyms and sports halls.

SPORTS GOVERNING BODIES — ELITE COMPETITOR — SCHOOL AND COMMUNITY — SPORTS CLUBS

FUNDING FOR SPORT

Issues In Sport

The Main Sources Of Income

Sport requires large amounts of money in order to operate.

NATIONAL LOTTERY SPORTS FUND
Began in 1994. Sport receives 5.6p from every £1 spent. Bids can be made for a lottery funding grant although they must fulfil certain criteria e.g. access for the disabled.

GOVERNMENT TAXES
National and Local Government raise money through taxation including gambling levies. Only a small amount of the money raised is given back to sport.

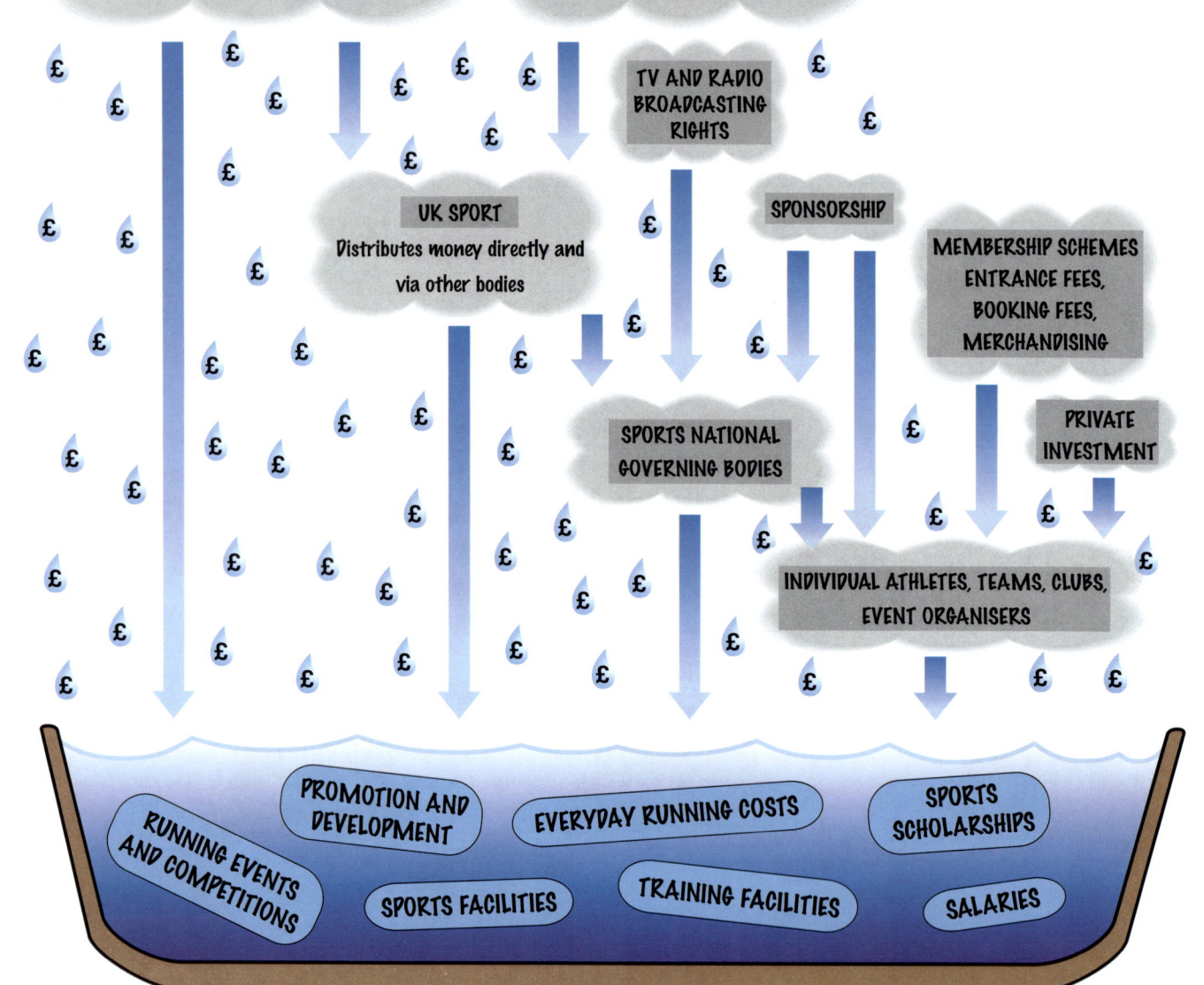

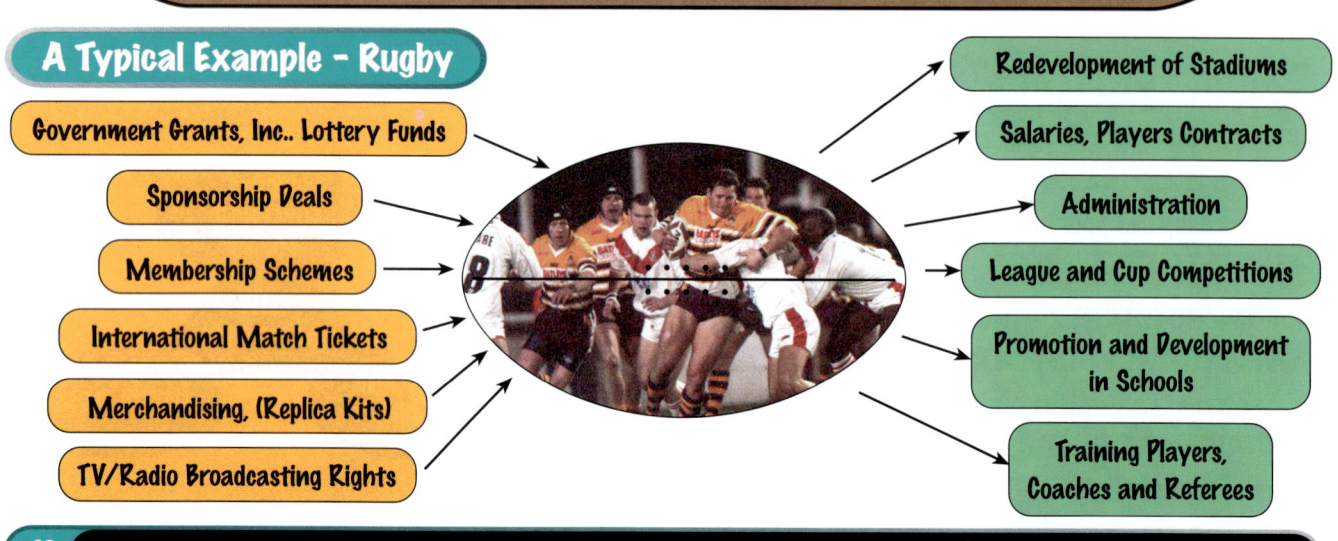

TV AND RADIO BROADCASTING RIGHTS

UK SPORT
Distributes money directly and via other bodies

SPONSORSHIP

MEMBERSHIP SCHEMES ENTRANCE FEES, BOOKING FEES, MERCHANDISING

SPORTS NATIONAL GOVERNING BODIES

PRIVATE INVESTMENT

INDIVIDUAL ATHLETES, TEAMS, CLUBS, EVENT ORGANISERS

- RUNNING EVENTS AND COMPETITIONS
- PROMOTION AND DEVELOPMENT
- EVERYDAY RUNNING COSTS
- SPORTS SCHOLARSHIPS
- SPORTS FACILITIES
- TRAINING FACILITIES
- SALARIES

A Typical Example – Rugby

Sources:
- Government Grants, Inc.. Lottery Funds
- Sponsorship Deals
- Membership Schemes
- International Match Tickets
- Merchandising, (Replica Kits)
- TV/Radio Broadcasting Rights

Uses:
- Redevelopment of Stadiums
- Salaries, Players Contracts
- Administration
- League and Cup Competitions
- Promotion and Development in Schools
- Training Players, Coaches and Referees

INTERNATIONAL SPORT I

Issues In Sport — 10

Major International Events

Major International events e.g. the OLYMPICS, WORLD CUP, WORLD CHAMPIONSHIPS attract worldwide PUBLIC INTEREST. Unfortunately they are often subject to POLITICAL and FINANCIAL PRESSURES.

POLITICAL - Furthering National ideals, Protests, Boycotts.

FINANCIAL - National debt, Over-commercialisation, Professionalism.

The Summer Olympic Games

The Summer Olympic games is the largest sporting event in the world. It takes place every four years and it is not without its fair share of controversy.

OLYMPIC IDEAL
"... not the winning but the taking part ... ... not the conquering, but fighting well ..."
Baron De Coubertain

1936 – BERLIN
- The games are used by Hitler to further the Nazi cause.
- He refuses to acknowledge the success of black US athlete Jesse Owens.

1972 – MUNICH
- Israeli athletes taken hostage by Palestinians.
- The failed rescue attempt results in the deaths of athletes, terrorists and police.

1980 – MOSCOW
- Boycott by some Western Nations, led by USA in protest of the USSR invasion of Afghanistan.
- UK athletes ignore government advice and compete.

1988 – SEOUL
- Ben Johnson stripped of 100m title and world record after testing positive for drugs.
- Boycott by North Korea.
- Tennis readmitted.

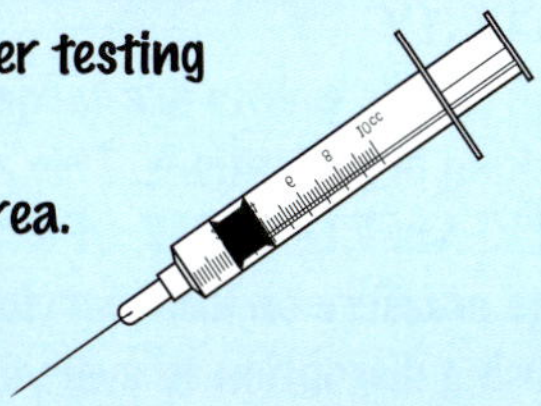

1968 – MEXICO CITY
- Black US athletes draw attention to civil rights problems in the USA by giving the 'Black Power' salute.
- South Africa refused admittance.

1976 – MONTREAL
- The city incurs huge financial debt.
- Boycott by many Black African countries protesting over New Zealand's rugby association with South Africa.

1984 – LOS ANGELES
- Boycott by USSR and its allies. Possible retaliation for 1980.
- Funded through sponsorship and TV rights. $235m profit. Some athletes 'paid,' (Amateur status was dropped in 1981).

1992 – BARCELONA
- Least controversial, a return to (some) Olympic ideals.
- South Africa readmitted and there is a unified German team.

Lonsdale School Revision Guides

69

INTERNATIONAL SPORT 2

Issues In Sport — 11

MAJOR INTERNATIONAL COMPETITIONS or EVENTS e.g. Olympics, World Cup, Grand Prix ...
... are arranged by INTERNATIONAL GOVERNING BODIES/ASSOCIATIONS e.g. IOC, FIFA, IAAF ...
... and are AWARDED to a HOST CITY or NATION by INTERNATIONAL COMMITTEES.

How Hosting Is Decided

A city or country (nation) can make a BID to the international committee and the successful host is announced FIVE years ahead of the event.

The international Committee will judge each bid on ...

... FACILITIES & INFRASTRUCTURE
- Venues
- Stadiums
- Accommodation
- Transport and Access (International and local)

... SECURITY
of the ...
- Competitors
- Spectators
- Officials
- Dignitaries

... DEVELOPMENT & PROMOTION
- Bringing sport to more people
- Encouraging International relations
- Cultural exchange

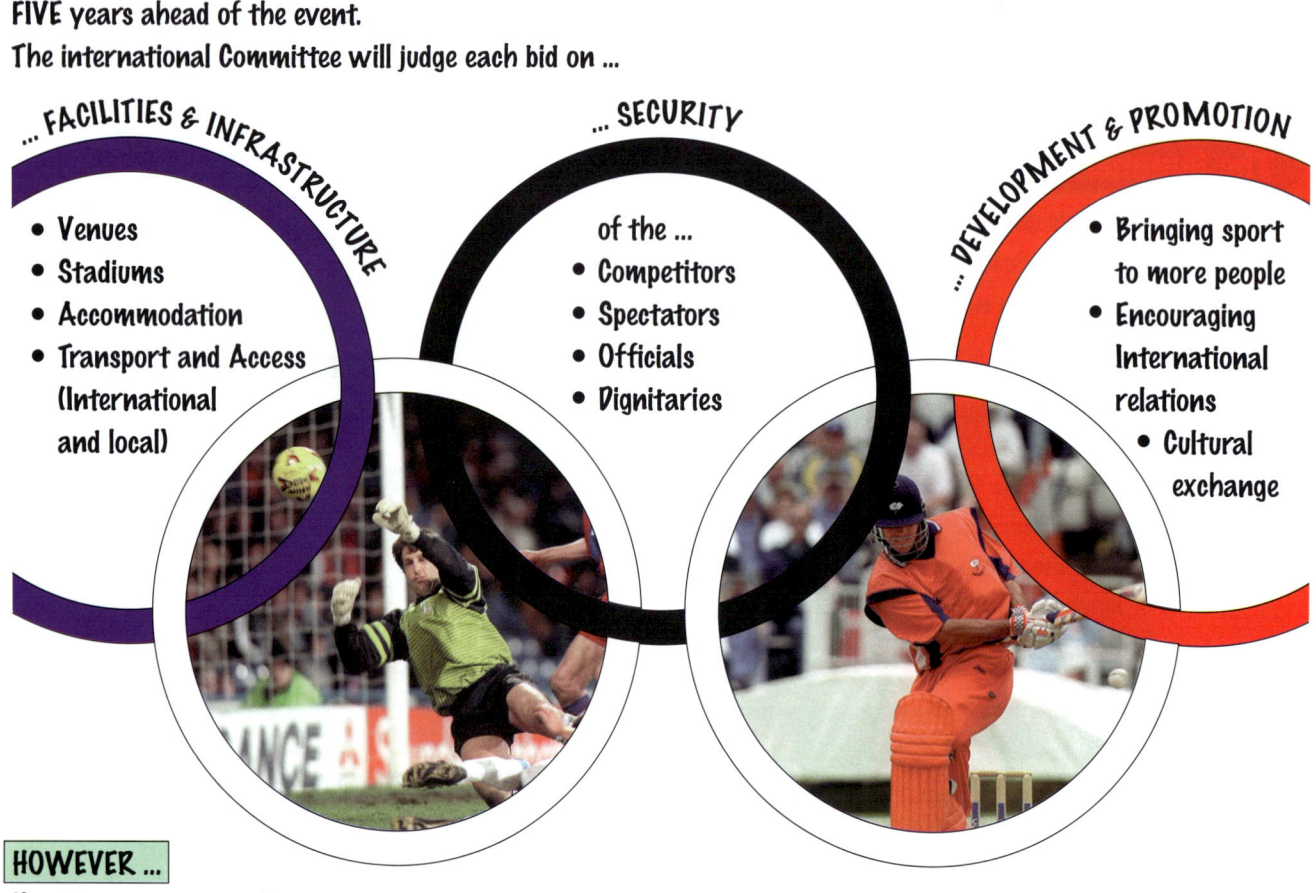

HOWEVER ...

Hosting an event can be a ...

... A BENEFIT 
1984 - LOS ANGELES OLYMPICS
$235m PROFIT

... A BURDEN 
1976 - MONTREAL OLYMPICS
$1 billion debt still being paid off!

Advantages And Disadvantages Of Hosting An Event

ADVANTAGES
- **INTERNATIONAL STATUS/RECOGNITION**
  Trade is boosted for many years after the event.
- **IMPROVED FACILITIES AND TRANSPORTATION**
  To benefit the local population after the event.
- **JOB CREATION**
  Building the facilities and staffing them.
- **MONEY MAKING**
  Organisers, local businesses and services.
- **CULTURAL EXCHANGE**
  Tourism is increased.

DISADVANTAGES
- **DEBT**
  Events are increasingly expensive to organise.
- **SECURITY**
  High profile events are targets for publicity seeking organisations. This adds to the cost.
- **INCREASED NUMBER OF VISITORS**
  Puts pressure on local service industries, causing disruption to everyday life.
- **SPECIALIST FACILITIES** - May become 'white elephants'.
- **MEDIA CRITICISM** - They will find something!

INTERNATIONAL SPORT 3

Issues In Sport — 12

Sport And Its Value To A Nation

All Governments want to encourage sporting excellence and achievement for their countries, since sport promotes ...

- ... INTERNATIONAL STATUS
- ... NATIONAL PRIDE
- ... A HEALTHY NATION
- ... NATIONAL UNITY
- ... SOCIAL INTEGRATION

Different countries use different approaches to promote sport at all levels.

UNITED KINGDOM

- Compulsory PE in state schools with some schools SPECIALISING.
- Clubs may have DEVELOPMENT SCHEMES for youth talent.
- Grants, scholarships, sponsorship for POTENTIAL ELITE.
- TRUST FUNDS for some elite competitors.
- SPORT FOR ALL CAMPAIGNS.

FORMER EASTERN BLOC

USSR, Romania, Poland, East Germany

- Sport was CONTROLLED and ENCOURAGED by the state to produce morale among the workforce and political prestige.
- Sports clubs linked with factories & Armed Forces.
- ELITE COMPETITORS nurtured from early age. They were then 'employed' by the state in industry or armed forces.
- Since 1989 more open professionalism.

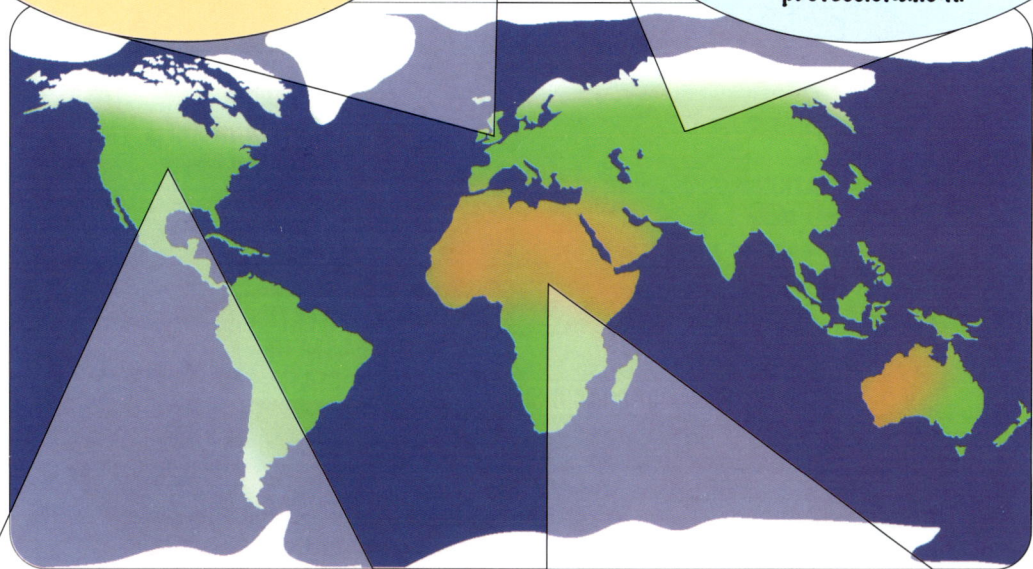

USA

- Compulsory PE in high schools with some schools SPECIALISING.
- School sport is very COMPETITIVE and HIGH PROFILE with much public interest.
- SCHOLARSHIPS to college or university and elite level coaching.
- NATIONWIDE INTEREST in college sport supported with TV and sponsorship money.
- DRAFT SYSTEM into PRO SPORT for top performers.

THE THIRD WORLD

Developing Nations in Africa (and Asia)

- LITTLE AVAILABLE MONEY means that sport must be CHEAP and POPULAR to develop.
- Athletics and football development are the most rapid.
- ELITE COMPETITORS supported by GOVERNMENT 'JOBS'.
- INTERNATIONAL SUCCESS brings in money!

THE ROLE OF THE SCHOOL IN PROMOTING PARTICIPATION

Participation In Sport — 1

Sport In School

Schools encourage participation in sport in a variety of ways such as performer, organiser, coach, captain, official (see MODES OF PARTICIPATION p. 76). This can lead to continued participation into adulthood, especially when links with sport clubs/ leisure centres are established.

Schools promote sport through PE and GAMES as:

COMPULSORY LESSONS	EXTRA CURRICULAR ACTIVITIES	AWARDS AND EXAMS
• National Curriculum (5-16 years) • Games, both team and individual • Gymnastics • Athletics • Dance • Swimming	• Representative teams • Sport Activity Clubs • Residential Holidays • Visits to Leisure centres • Links with Local Clubs • Specialist Coaching Clinics	• Sport Specific Achievement Awards/Certificates e.g. BAGA, ASA • Sports Leaders Awards • GCSE Level Exam • 'A' Level Exam • GNVQ

Activities Available For School Children

These depend on ...

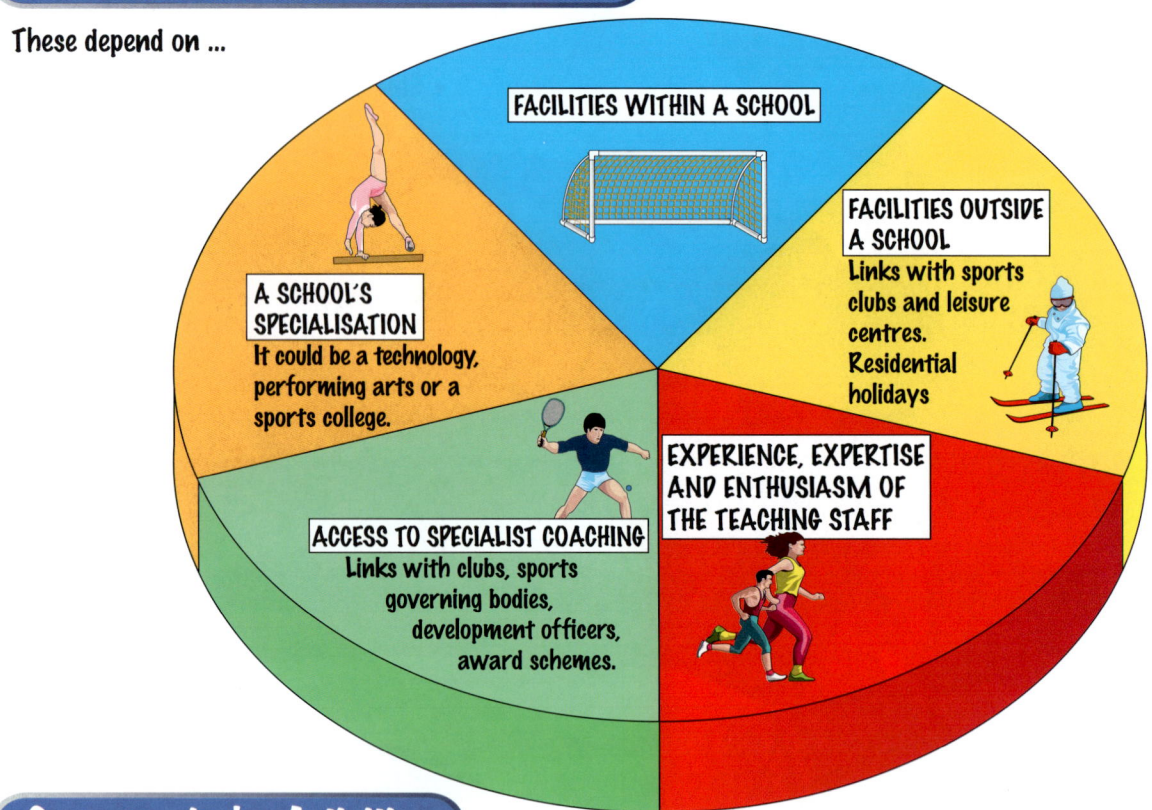

- **FACILITIES WITHIN A SCHOOL**
- **FACILITIES OUTSIDE A SCHOOL** — Links with sports clubs and leisure centres. Residential holidays
- **EXPERIENCE, EXPERTISE AND ENTHUSIASM OF THE TEACHING STAFF**
- **ACCESS TO SPECIALIST COACHING** — Links with clubs, sports governing bodies, development officers, award schemes.
- **A SCHOOL'S SPECIALISATION** — It could be a technology, performing arts or a sports college.

Cross-curricular Activities

Schools also promote HEALTH EDUCATION in other lessons across the curriculum in ...

... PSE, SCIENCE, FOOD TECHNOLOGY, DRAMA, ICT (key skills) and HEALTH AWARENESS DAYS.

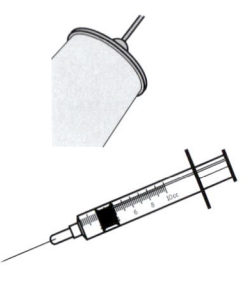

CROSS-CURRICULAR THEMES INCLUDE ...
- Diet
- Personal Hygiene
- Health and Fitness
- Drugs Awareness
- Social Relationships

Changing Attitudes I – SOCIAL CHANGE

Participation In Sport — 2

Sport For The Masses

Sport reflects society. As society has evolved and changed in the last one hundred and fifty years so has its attitude towards sport and physical recreation.

Gone are the days where sport was seen as a privilege of the chosen few as today a wide variety of sporting activities are available to everybody.

Sport for a few in the 19th Century

MOST ORGANISED SPORT WAS ...
- ... the privilege of the wealthy upper classes.
- ... seen as a hobby or pastime.
- ... mostly amateur ('Gentlemen').
- ... limited by choice of activity.
- ... not available to most of the lower classes due to widespread poverty.

REASONS FOR EVOLUTION OF SOCIAL CHANGE

- STATE EDUCATION FOR ALL
- BETTER WORKING CONDITIONS
- WEALTH MORE EVENLY DISTRIBUTED
- EVOLUTION OF PROFESSIONAL SPORT AND ELITISM
- RECOGNITION OF THE BENEFITS OF PHYSICAL RECREATION
- BETTER HEALTHCARE
- COMMERCIAL INVOLVEMENT
- TECHNOLOGICAL DEVELOPMENTS IN TRANSPORT AND COMMUNICATION

TODAY ...
- ... provision of facilities in schools, communities is better.
- ... physical recreation is promoted for a healthy lifestyle.
- ... amateurism exists mostly at recreational levels.
- ... professionalism has meant improved competition.
- ... there is increased participation in all social groups: women, disabled, juniors, veterans.
- ... there are many career opportunities due to the growth of the sport, fitness and leisure industry.

Sport for all in the 21st Century

Changing Attitudes 2 – WOMEN AND THE DISABLED
Participation In Sport — 3

Women In Sport And Physical Recreation

OLD TRADITIONAL VIEW WAS THAT …
- … physical activity was masculine.
- … family responsibilities came first.
- … physical activity was harmful to the anatomy.
- … there was a limited range of activities available.
- … women's sport lacks media attention.
- … sport is male dominated.

REASONS FOR EVOLUTION OF SOCIAL CHANGE

TODAY …
- … there is a wider range of sporting activities/opportunities available.
- … barriers to traditional sports are being removed. e.g. football, rugby, cricket.
- … Womens Sports Foundation has resulted in a greater involvement in administration, coaching, management and the media.
- … women's sport in the USA is a growth industry!

THE SEX DISCRIMINATION ACT EMPHASISED WOMENS RIGHTS.

MEN ADOPTING MORE DOMESTIC RESPONSIBILITIES

THE EQUAL OPPORTUNITY ACT HAS REDEFINED THEIR STATUS IN SOCIETY.

IMPROVED PROVISION OF FACILITIES e.g. CRÈCHES AT SPORTS CENTRES, WOMEN ONLY SESSIONS.

The Disabled In Sport And Physical Recreation

Society now focuses on what the disabled CAN DO rather than what they cannot do.
Greater provision for the disabled athlete is made through DISABILITY SPORT ENGLAND (1994). These include:

- Improved access to more sports
- More involvement with 'fully abled'
- Competitions for the disabled
- Improved access to sports centres etc
- Sports planning now include the disabled
- Recognition of their sporting abilities
- Media coverage raises awareness
- Recognition of their needs
- Lighter materials available e.g. for wheelchairs

Changing Attitudes 3 – ENCOURAGING PARTICIPATION
Participation In Sport — 4

Encouraging Participation

The government now recognises the benefits of Physical Recreation. Its policy is to encourage greater participation in sport and physical activity. This is achieved through a partnership between:

LOCAL AUTHORITIES
They encourage participation through …
… the provision of PUBLIC FACILITIES …
… the 'DUAL USE' of SCHOOL FACILITIES …
… and the organisation of 'SPECIAL SESSIONS' at SPORTS CENTRES.
e.g. reduced daytime rates for the unemployed, women only sessions and over 50's sessions.

GOVERNING BODIES
They encourage participation through …
… DEVELOPMENT SCHEMES from 'grass roots' through to 'elite' levels, …
… and UK SPORT and the HOME COUNTRY COUNCILS e.g. SPORT ENGLAND.

The Role Of The Sports Councils

UK Sport and the Home Country Councils have many roles (see p.83). One of their roles is to encourage participation at all levels. They do this by IDENTIFYING PROBLEMS and then PRESENTING SOLUTIONS.

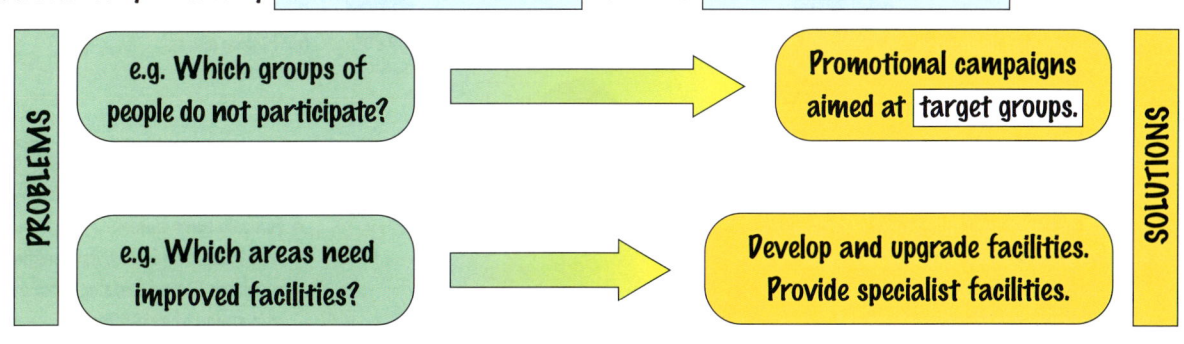

PROBLEMS
- e.g. Which groups of people do not participate?
- e.g. Which areas need improved facilities?

SOLUTIONS
- Promotional campaigns aimed at target groups.
- Develop and upgrade facilities. Provide specialist facilities.

Examples of PROMOTIONAL CAMPAIGNS have been …

- **1981** – 'SPORT FOR ALL' – DISABLED PEOPLE
- **1983** – 50+ 'ALL TO PLAY FOR'
- **1985** – 13-24 AGE GROUP 'EVER THOUGHT OF SPORT?'
- **1987** – 13-24, 45-49 AGE GROUP WOMEN 'WHAT'S YOUR SPORT?'
- **1988** – 'WHAT'S YOUR SPORT?' FOR WOMEN
- **1989** – WOMEN 'MILK IN ACTION'
- **1991** – 'YEAR OF SPORT'

Overall there has been a moderate increase in the level of participation. Women's football is one activity where participation is growing as women enjoy greater freedom of choice.

However … participation in some sports may decline. Snooker and squash are now less fashionable while some activities may be seen as expensive and therefore dependent on individual wealth, e.g. sailing, winter sports (skiing and snowboarding).

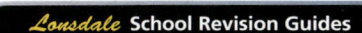

MODES OF PARTICIPATION

Participation In Sport — 5

Participation In Sport

Participation in sport or physical recreation is for one of three main reasons...
HEALTH, **LEISURE** or **VOCATIONAL**.

A person can participate in many different ways ...

PLAYER/PERFORMER
- Recreational, part or full time professional.
- Qualifications? (talent, ability, commitment)

ADMINISTRATOR/ORGANISER
- To run the club, organisation.
- Full, part or spare time.
- Chairperson, Accountant, Office staff.
- Professional (business) qualifications required.

OFFICIAL
- Referees, judges, umpires, linespersons.
- Full, part or spare time.
- Qualifications and experience required for higher levels.

GROUNDS MAN/WOMAN
- Maintenance of sports surfaces.
- Becoming increasingly specialised and technical.
- Qualifications - experience and dedication.

COACH/INSTRUCTOR/TRAINER
- Full, part or spare time.
- Work with all levels of ability (beginners to professional).
- Qualifications and experience required for higher levels.

CHOREOGRAPHER
- Dance teachers and movement coordinators.
- Work in many sports as well as dance e.g. tennis, ice skating.
- Professional qualifications required.

PE TEACHER
- Full and part time.
- Professional and specialist qualifications required: Degree and Coaching awards in a range of activities.

Other Careers Related To Sport

MEDIA	SPORTS MEDICINE/SCIENCE	DEVELOPMENT OFFICERS	PHYSICAL TRAINING INSTRUCTORS (PTI's)
• Journalists • Reporters • Broadcasters • Photographers • Technicians	• Physiotherapists • Sports injury clinics • Training method research	• Sports promotion at 'grass roots.'	• Armed Forces • Police • Fire Service

LEISURE INDUSTRY
- Leisure centres employ Managers, Instructors, Lifeguards, Attendants, Activity leaders.
- National parks, Activity centres employ Wardens, Rangers.
- Tourism - activity and adventure holidays employ administrators, leaders.
- Clothing and equipment manufacture and retail.
- Personal Trainers.

FACTORS AFFECTING PARTICIPATION

Participation In Sport — 6

Everyone is subject to FACTORS which may influence their PARTICIPATION in a sport or activity.

Social Groupings

FAMILY
Provide...
- Early introduction to activities.
- Role models (parent and siblings).
- Encouragement and support.

GENDER
- Male participation is higher than female.
- More sports and activities are available to males.

PEERS
Friends of similar age or background can be...
- Active – teams, clubs.
- Non-active who view sport as 'uncool' or a 'waste of time.'

GROUP PRESSURE EXERTED BY THESE CAN BE...

...POSITIVE
- Active
- Supportive
- Supportive
- Encouraging
- Role models

...NEGATIVE
- Non-active
- Alternative interests
- External interests high
- Too masculine or feminine
- Cultural differences

RACE, TRADITION, CULTURE
In some countries...
- 'National sports' are more popular.
- Sport is important and sportsmen/women have a high profile.
- Women's sport is still disapproved of.

POPULARITY
- Football is well promoted, advertised.
- It has high profile role models
- Requires little equipment or organisation at basic level.

SOCIO-ECONOMIC
- Unemployment limits participation due to lack of money.
- Some sports are too expensive.
- Local communities or countries may be too poor to provide facilities.

Other Factors

AGE
- Some sports or activities are more appropriate to certain age groups.
- People may participate less and in fewer activities the older they get.

DISABILITY
- This may limit the number and type of sports available and who you can participate with.
- Many sports are doing more to provide for disabled athletes.

ACCESS
- Depends on how near you live to a sports facility.

ENVIRONMENT/CLIMATE
- Top 'winter sports' people tend to come from cold, mountainous regions/environments.

POLITICS
- Government involvement on how much is spent on providing facilities for public use.
- The 'Elite' may receive special help to promote excellence and national pride.

MEDIA
- Can raise awareness of sports, activities and healthy lifestyles.
- Promote role models.
- Increase the popularity of minority sports.

EDUCATION
- A positive school experience may lead to continued participation in later life.
- Compulsory PE in state schools up to 16 years.

TYPES OF COMPETITION

Participation In Sport — 7

Ladder

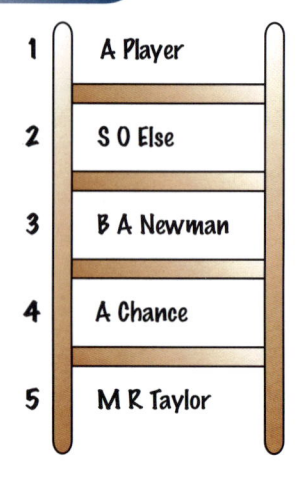

1. A Player
2. S O Else
3. B A Newman
4. A Chance
5. M R Taylor

- Usually employed in badminton, tennis and squash clubs enabling players of similar ability to play competitively.

- A player can challenge the player above and if successful take over the higher place.

- In some cases a player can challenge a player up to 3 places above. A successful challenge would result in all the players in between also moving down one place, as the winner takes over the higher place.

League

- Each team must play a fixture against every other team, usually at 'home' and 'away'.

- Points are awarded for winning eg. 3 pts and for drawing e.g. 1 pt.

- Teams level on points may be separated by 'goal difference'.

- Sports such as Rugby may use the difference between 'points scored' and 'points conceded'.

ACME B MID-CHESHIRE MOTORWAY LEAGUE

		P	W	L	D	F	A	PTS
1	Sandbach	8	7	0	1	24	8	22
2	Middlewich	8	6	2	0	25	11	18
3	Kidsgrove	8	5	1	2	19	8	17
4	Biddulph	8	5	2	1	20	9	16
5	Alsager	8	4	2	2	16	13	14
6	Knutsford	8	4	3	1	14	13	13
7	Northwich	8	4	4	0	17	19	12
8	Sale	8	2	1	5	11	12	11
9	Alderley	8	3	3	2	10	14	11
10	Stockton	8	1	5	2	6	17	5

Knock Out

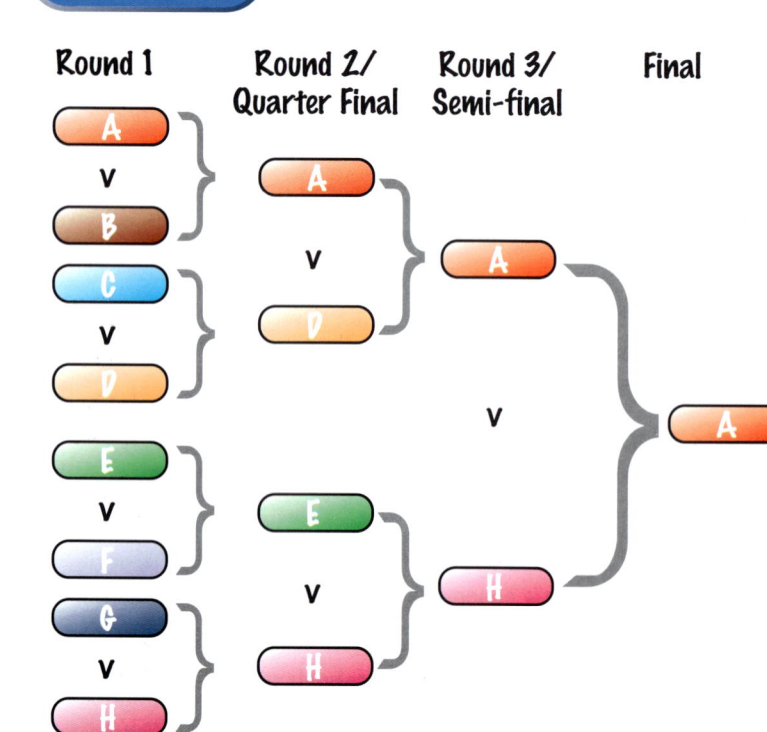

Round 1 / Round 2 / Quarter Final / Round 3 / Semi-final / Final

- Usually involves a 'draw' to see who plays against whom eg. FA Cup.

- The 'draw' may be 'seeded' to prevent the better players/teams eliminating each other too early in the competition. This should ensure even competition in the latter stages eg. Tennis tournaments.

78

Lonsdale School Revision Guides

LEISURE TIME

• Participation In Sport **8**

Leisure Time

Leisure time is SPARE TIME to spend as you please, away from work and other commitments. Continuing improvements in TECHNOLOGY has created INCREASED LEISURE TIME for many people. More MECHANISATION and COMPUTERISATION means ...

... AT WORK
- Jobs are becoming ...
  ... less physically demanding.
- More flexible working hours.
- More part-time work.
- More people are taking ...
  ... early retirement.

... AT HOME
- Labour saving devices ...
  ... are reducing time spent ...
  ... on domestic chores.
- People can work from home ...
  ... saving on travelling time.
- Home shopping and banking ...
  ... via the TV, telephone and internet.
- Convenience cooking.

The Leisure Industry

Increased leisure time has led to a growth in the LEISURE INDUSTRY.
Providers of leisure facilities fall into three categories:

1. THE PRIVATE SECTOR
- Leisure facilities controlled and run by the Private Sector are many.
  Each one has one purpose only ... to make MONEY! Typical examples are ...

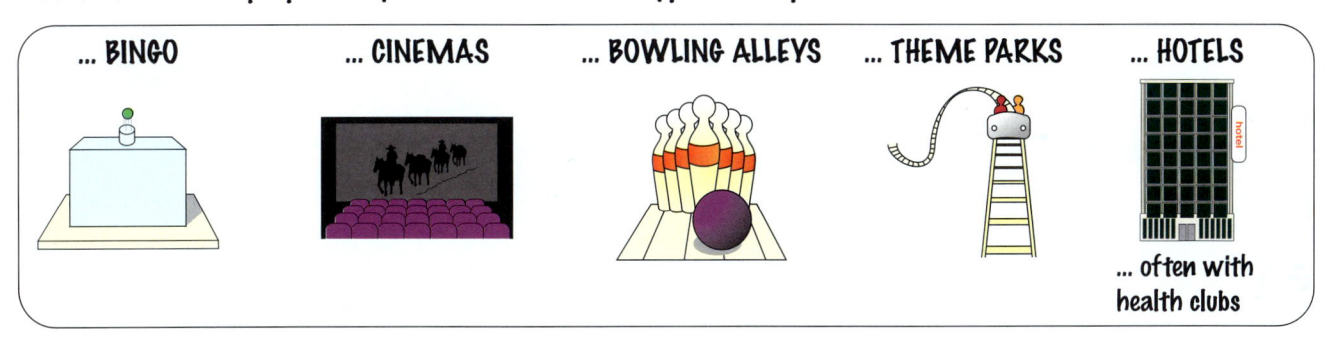

... BINGO   ... CINEMAS   ... BOWLING ALLEYS   ... THEME PARKS   ... HOTELS
... often with health clubs

2. LOCAL AUTHORITIES
- Leisure facilities controlled and run by Local Authorities are NON-PROFIT making. Typical examples are ...

... LEISURE CENTRES   ... PARKS   ... GARDENS   ... MUSEUMS   ... SWIMMING POOLS

Also ... Local Authority run facilities often have CONCESSIONARY PRICES for the UNEMPLOYED and OLDER PEOPLE during OFF-PEAK times. These groups have more leisure time but less disposable income to spend on leisure activities.

3. VOLUNTARY ORGANISATIONS
- These are also NON-PROFIT making. Examples include YOUTH CLUBS, the NATIONAL TRUST and various COMMON INTEREST GROUPS.

PROVISION FOR EXCELLENCE I

Participation In Sport — 9

The structure of sport must assist and support the DEVELOPMENT of talented INDIVIDUALS, TEAMS and SQUADS from 'GRASS ROOTS' level through to the potential 'ELITE PERFORMER'.

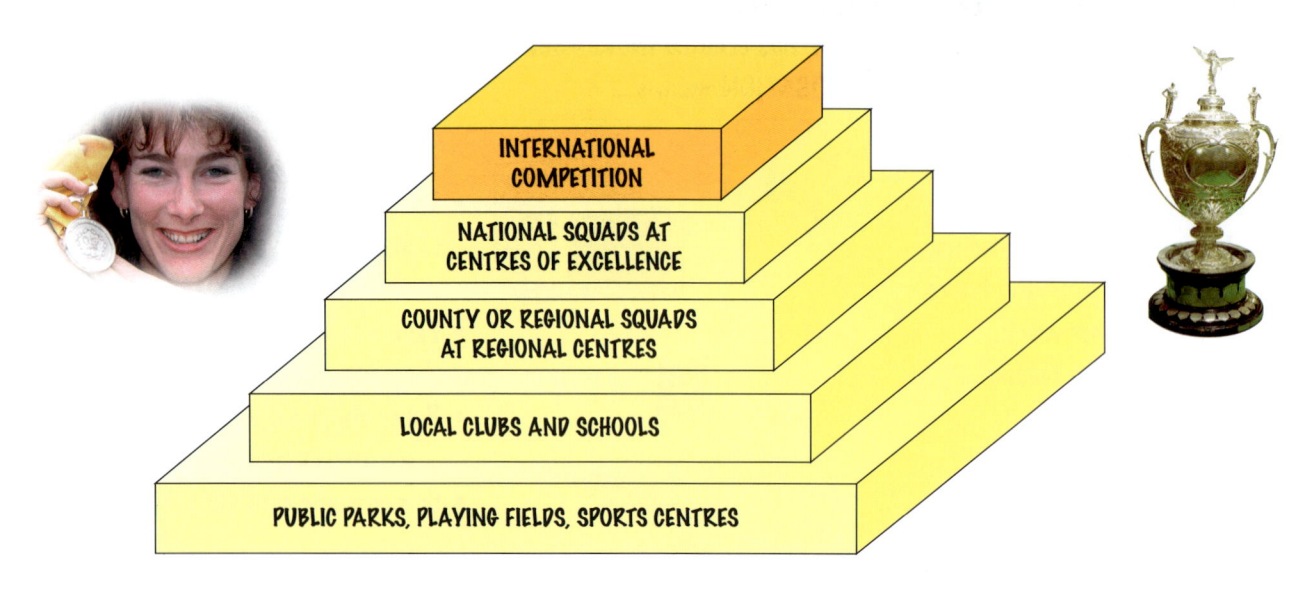

Pyramid (top to bottom):
- INTERNATIONAL COMPETITION
- NATIONAL SQUADS AT CENTRES OF EXCELLENCE
- COUNTY OR REGIONAL SQUADS AT REGIONAL CENTRES
- LOCAL CLUBS AND SCHOOLS
- PUBLIC PARKS, PLAYING FIELDS, SPORTS CENTRES

In order to achieve excellence at all levels then good COACHING, FACILITIES and FUNDING are required.

Coaching

Good quality coaching is vital at all levels to support development. It may be provided by...

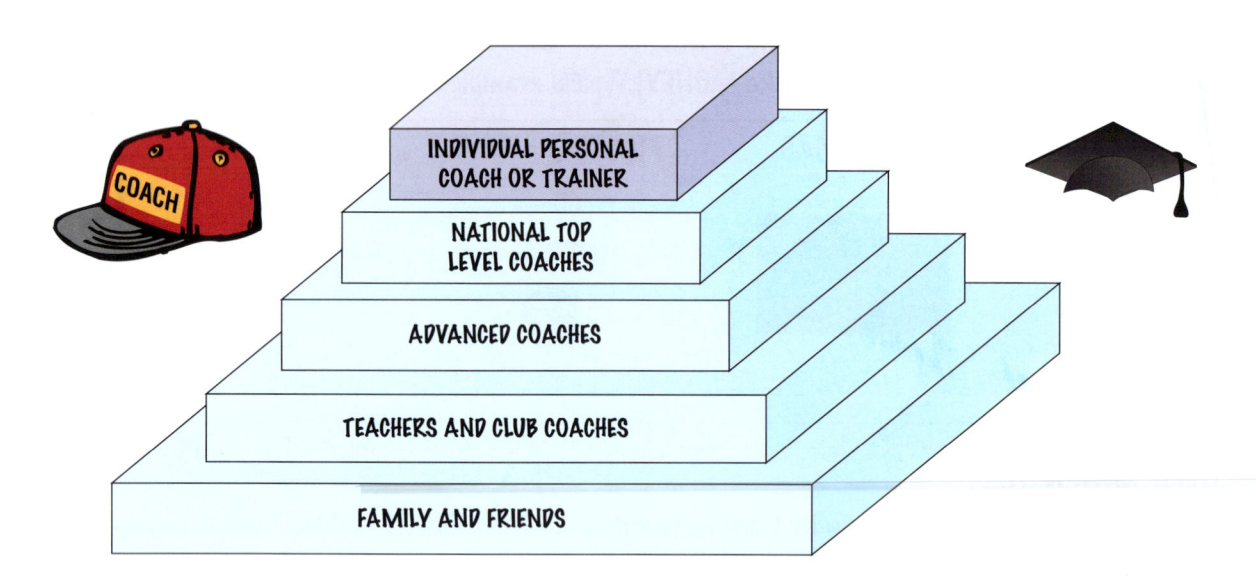

Pyramid (top to bottom):
- INDIVIDUAL PERSONAL COACH OR TRAINER
- NATIONAL TOP LEVEL COACHES
- ADVANCED COACHES
- TEACHERS AND CLUB COACHES
- FAMILY AND FRIENDS

UK Sport (formerly the Sports Council) created the NATIONAL COACHING FOUNDATION to co-ordinate and improve coaching for user groups of ALL AGES both individual and team. It involves...

COACH DEVELOPMENT PROGRAMME
- Introduction to Diploma level qualifications.
- Resources and information service.
- National Coaching Centres at Universities and Colleges.

YOUTH SPORT TRUST
- A fun and successful introduction to sport.
- Programmes for 4-11 year olds.
- 'Bringing Sport to Life for Young People.'
- A registered charity.

CHAMPION COACHING
- Quality Coaching for 11-16 year olds.
- Progression from schools to clubs.
- Recruitment and development of coaches.

IMPROVED TECHNICAL SUPPORT
- Personal Coach.
- Sports Medicine.
- Sports Science.

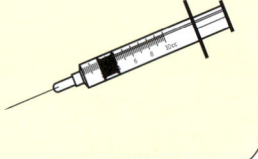

PROVISION FOR EXCELLENCE 2

Participation In Sport — 10

Facilities

There are twelve National Sports Centres in the UK.

These **CENTRES OF EXCELLENCE** are used...

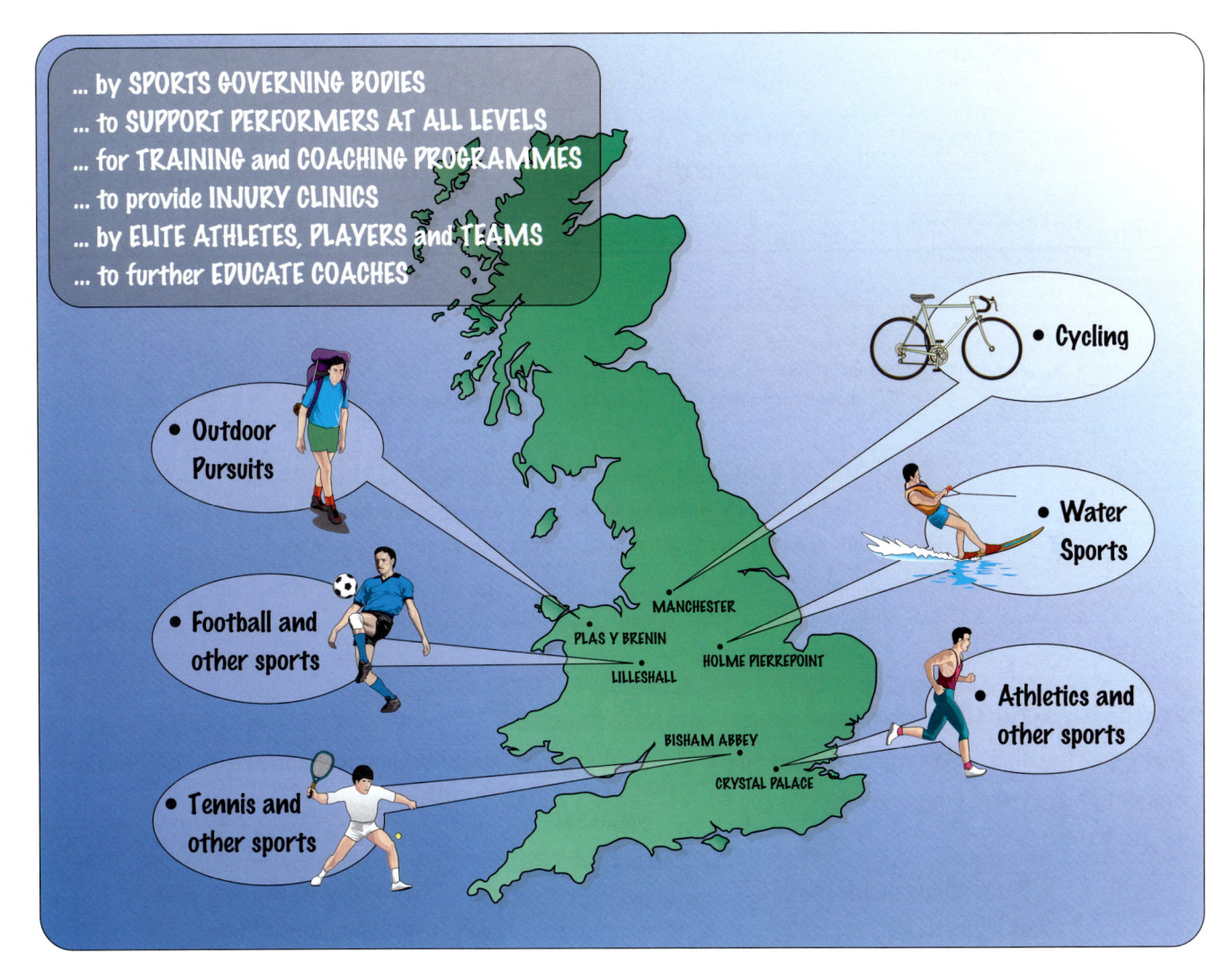

... by SPORTS GOVERNING BODIES
... to SUPPORT PERFORMERS AT ALL LEVELS
... for TRAINING and COACHING PROGRAMMES
... to provide INJURY CLINICS
... by ELITE ATHLETES, PLAYERS and TEAMS
... to further EDUCATE COACHES

- Cycling
- Outdoor Pursuits
- Water Sports
- Football and other sports
- Athletics and other sports
- Tennis and other sports

MANCHESTER
PLAS Y BRENIN
HOLME PIERREPOINT
LILLESHALL
BISHAM ABBEY
CRYSTAL PALACE

The UK Institute of Sport (proposed) will be a NETWORK of facilities based on the Centres of Excellence.

Funding

SPORTS AID, formerly called Sports Aid Foundation was set up to ...

... **DEVELOP EXCELLENCE** by helping elite athletes to prepare for and compete in International Events

... **ENCOURAGE TALENT** by helping disabled athletes and talented youngsters achieve their potential.

It raises money from SPONSORSHIP, LOCAL AUTHORITIES and CHARITIES.
Money is then distributed through GOVERNING BODIES in the form of grants.

HOWEVER

- Many athletes work hard to find their own sponsorship or they fund themselves through part time work. In many cases parents and families often provide financial support.

THE FRAMEWORK, STRUCTURE & ORGANISATION OF SPORT IN THE UK • Participation In Sport

The Basic Framework Of Sport In The U.K.

TO DEVELOP and FUNCTION different sports must be part of a National Framework of Sports Organisations, which are effectively STRUCTURED and well MANAGED. Central to all of this are the NATIONAL GOVERNING BODIES.

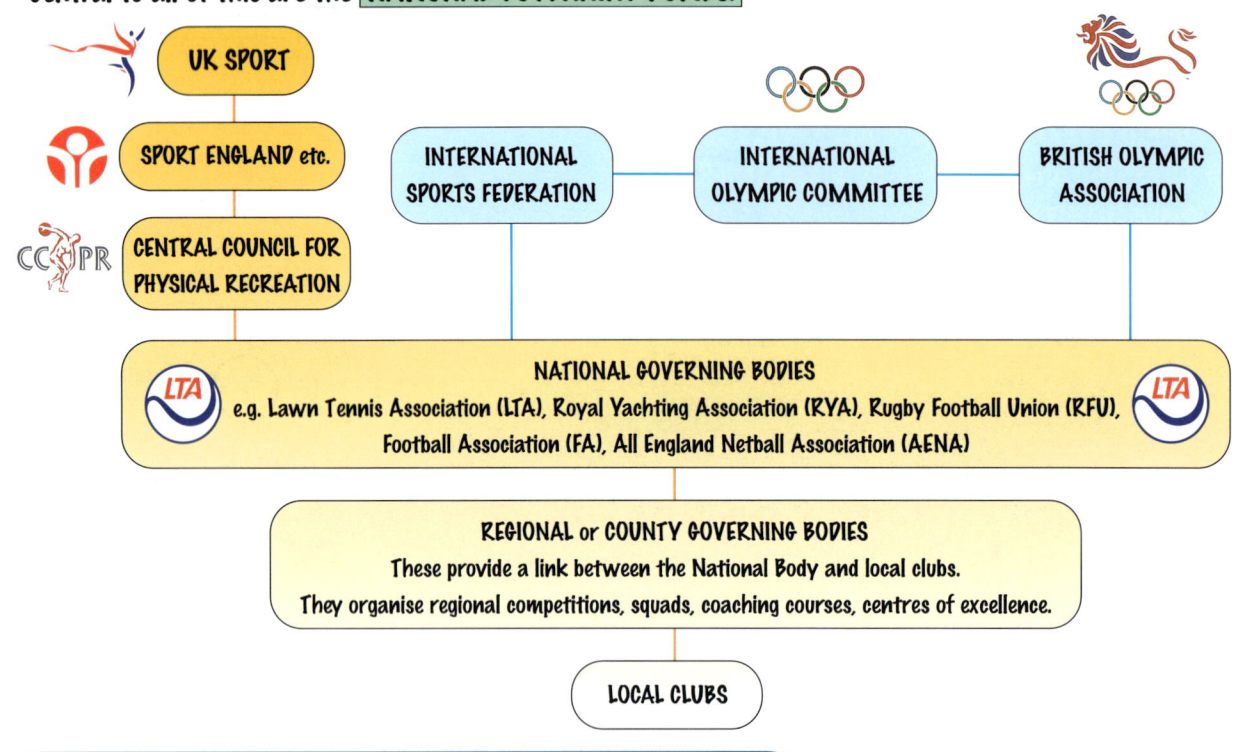

- UK SPORT
- SPORT ENGLAND etc.
- CENTRAL COUNCIL FOR PHYSICAL RECREATION

- INTERNATIONAL SPORTS FEDERATION
- INTERNATIONAL OLYMPIC COMMITTEE
- BRITISH OLYMPIC ASSOCIATION

NATIONAL GOVERNING BODIES
e.g. Lawn Tennis Association (LTA), Royal Yachting Association (RYA), Rugby Football Union (RFU), Football Association (FA), All England Netball Association (AENA)

REGIONAL or COUNTY GOVERNING BODIES
These provide a link between the National Body and local clubs.
They organise regional competitions, squads, coaching courses, centres of excellence.

LOCAL CLUBS

Responsibilities And Duties Of A Governing Body

Every sport in this country is controlled by its own GOVERNING BODY which has many responsibilities and duties. A typical Governing Body is the LAWN TENNIS ASSOCIATION (LTA).

LAWN TENNIS ASSOCIATION, LTA

- Encouraging participants at all levels.
- Training referees and umpires.
- Setting down rules and laws, overseeing any changes.
- Developing young TALENT to their full potential e.g. 'Rover Junior Squads'.
- Selecting and preparing National squads e.g. 'Davis' and 'Federation' Cup teams.
- Linking with the International Governing Bodies.
- Distributing funds to local clubs.
- Raising funds through subscriptions, sponsorship, ticket sales, broadcasting rights.
- Arranging competitions at Local and National level e.g. RATINGS TOURNAMENTS which provide scope for a range of challenge for all abilities.
  - All players receive a 'RATING' according to ability.
  - They enter a tournament at the appropriate level.
  - Ratings can go up or down if they win or lose.
  - Funded by sponsorship and entry fees.
- Developing EXCELLENCE by providing facilities, coaching and funding for ELITE players.

ORGANISATIONS INFLUENCING PARTICIPATION I

Participation In Sport — 12

The Sports Councils

UK SPORT (formerly known as the Sports Council) is an organisation which deals with the development of sport and sporting performance in the U.K. as a whole. Each home country also has its own sports council ...
... SPORT ENGLAND, SPORT SCOTLAND, SPORTS COUNCIL FOR WALES and SPORTS COUNCIL FOR N. IRELAND.

UK SPORT and the HOME COUNTRY COUNCILS

The key roles of UK SPORT are to:
- Support elite performers.
- Oversee doping control, ethics and sports science.
- Promote international status by attracting major events e.g. world cups.
- Co-ordinate all organisations within the national framework.

The key roles of the HOME COUNTRY COUNCILS are to:
- Increase participation.
- Improve the number and quality of facilities available.
- Raise standards and develop excellence.
- Allocate Lottery funding.

Central Council For Physical Recreation

The CENTRAL COUNCIL FOR PHYSICAL RECREATION (CCPR) is an organisation with more than 300 Sports Governing Bodies as its members. Each member belongs to one or more of the following sub-divisions.

| GAMES AND SPORTS | MAJOR SPECTATOR SPORTS | MOVEMENT AND DANCE | OUTDOOR PURSUITS | WATER RECREATION | OTHER INTERESTED ORGANISATIONS |

The key roles of CCPR are to:
- Represents its members on appropriate sports councils.
- Promote sport participation.
- Promote campaigns for 'Fair Play in Sport' and against 'Drugs in Sport'.
- Liaise with Central and Local Government, Media, Sponsors.
- Develop award schemes e.g. Community Sports Leaders (16+).

NB The BRITISH SPORTS TRUST was set up by CCPR as a registered charity. It trains people of all ages to be leaders in their community. It does this through a scheme called the SPORTS LEADER AWARDS.

ORGANISATIONS INFLUENCING PARTICIPATION 2

International Olympic Committee

The INTERNATIONAL OLYMPIC COMMITTEE (IOC) is the supreme power responsible for events connected with the OLYMPIC GAMES. It consists of representatives of Olympic Associations from various countries and the International Sports Federation (ISF).

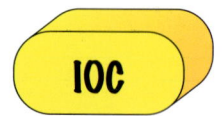

The key roles of the IOC are to:
- Select venues i.e. the host cities and plan the games in conjunction with the hosts and ISF.
- Approve the sports to take place in the games.
- Promote sporting ethics e.g. fair play, non-use of drugs.
- Promote sport development and participation around the world.
- Oppose political and commercial abuse.

British Olympic Association

The BRITISH OLYMPIC ASSOCIATION (BOA) is responsible for events connected with the OLYMPIC GAMES in GREAT BRITAIN.

The key roles of the BOA are to:
- Choose the British team for the games and organise their preparation and participation.
- Assist with technical and financial support.
- Foster the Olympic ideals and movement.
- Raise money without political involvement.
- Promote participation at all levels.

Countryside Agency

The COUNTRYSIDE AGENCY (formerly known as the Countryside Commission) is responsible for the ENGLISH COUNTRYSIDE. The other Home countries have their own organisations.

The key roles of the COUNTRYSIDE AGENCY are to:
- Maintain, conserve and run the National parks e.g. Lake District, North Yorks Moors, Peak District, Dartmoor.
- Give the Government guidance on policy and management.
- Maintain trails, footpaths and free access.
- Promote recreation and understanding.
- Monitor the impact various activities have.

INDEX

A

ABC Procedure 45, 49
Adrenalin 19
Aerobic Fitness 30
Aerobic Respiration 17
Aerobic Training 30
Age 54
Aggression 55
Agility 39
Alcohol 56
Amateurs 65
Anabolic Agents 56
Anaerobic Fitness 30
Anaerobic Respiration 18
Anaerobic Training 30
Arteries 11, 12
Assessment 58
Athletic Activities 42

B

Balance 39
Basal Metabolic Rate 20
Beta Blockers 56
Blood 11, 12
Blood Doping 56
Blood Pressure 13
Blood Vessels 11, 12
Bones 5, 6
Breathing 15
British Olympic Association 82, 84
Bruising 48

C

Capillaries 11, 12
Carbohydrates 15, 21, 22
Carbon Dioxide 14
Cardiac Massage 47
Cardiac Muscles 9
Cardiac Output 13
Cardiorespiratory System 36
Cardiovascular System 36
Cartilage 6
Cells 15
Central Council For Physical Recreation 82, 83
Circuit Training 31
Circulatory System 11, 35

Clothing 59
Coaching 80
Coordination 39
Competitions 78
Concussion 49
Continuous Training 33
Cooper Test 38
Core Temperature 37
Countryside Agency 84
Cramp 50
Cross-curricular Activities 72
Cuts 50
Cycle Ergonometer Test 38

D

Dance 42
Dehydration 50
Diastolic Pressure 13
Diet 21, 22
Digital Cameras 59
Disability 74
Dislocations 49
Diuretics 56
Dynamic Strength 25, 26

E

Ectomorph 53
Endomorph 53
Energy 15
Energy Balance 20
Equipment 59
Exercise 23, 36
Explosive Strength 25, 26

F

Facilities 66, 80, 81
Factors Affecting Participation 77
Factors Affecting Performance 51, 52, 53, 54, 55, 56, 57, 58
Fartlek Training 33
Fast Twitch Fibres 10, 27
Fats 21, 22
Feedback 58
Fibre 21
Fitness 4
Fitness Tests 27, 39
Flexibility 28, 29
Footcare 43

Footwear 41, 59
Fractures 49
Funding 68, 80, 81

G

Game Activities 42
Gender 54
General Fitness 4
Glucose 15
Glycogen 15
Governing Bodies 75, 82
Grazes 50
Guidance 57
Gymnastic Activities 42

H

Harvard Step Test 38
Health 4
Heart 11
Heart Rate 13
Heart Rate Monitors 59
Heat Exhaustion 50
Heat Stroke 50
Hormones 56
Hormonal System 19
Hypothermia 50

I

ICT 59
Injury 40
Insulin 19
International Olympic Committee 82, 84
International Sport 69, 70, 71
International Sports Federation 82
Interval Training 32
Involuntary Muscles 9
Isometric Contraction 10
Isotonic Contraction 10

J

Joints 6, 7, 8
Joints, Movement 7, 8

K

Knock Out 78

INDEX

L

Ladders 78
Leagues 78
Leisure Industry 79
Leisure Time 79
Lifestyle 54
Liver 15
Local Authorities 75
Lungs 11, 14

M

Media 62, 63
Media Coverage 62, 63
Mental Well-being 23
Mesomorph 53
Minute Volume 15
Motor Fitness 4
Mouth To Mouth Resuscitation 46, 47
Multi-Stage Fitness Test 38
Muscle System 35
Muscles 9, 10
Muscle Contraction 10
Muscular Endurance 25, 26
Muscular Strength 25

N

Narcotic Analgesics 56
Nervous System 19

O

Olympic Games 69
Overload 24
Oxygen 14, 17
Oxygen Debt 18

P

Participation 76, 77
Periodisation 34
Personal Hygiene 43
Personality 55
Physical Exercise 4
Physical Well-being 23
Plasma 12
Platelets 12
Posture 44

Power 39
Power Analysis 59
Practice 57
Pressure Training 33
Professionals 65
Progression 24
Protein 21, 22
Providers 66
Pulse 13

R

R.I.C.E Treatment 48
Reaction Time 39
Recovery Position 45, 46, 47
Red Cells 12
Respiration 15, 36
Respiratory Rate 15
Respiratory system 35
Reversibility 24

S

Safety 42
School 72
Seasonal Sport 34
Semi-Professionals 65
Shock 50
Skeletal Muscle 15
Skeletal System 35
Skeleton 5
Skill 57
Slow Twitch Fibres 10, 27
Social Change 73, 74
Social Well-being 23
Somatotypes 53
Specificity 24
Speed 27
Sponsorship 60, 61
Sport England 82, 83
Sporting Behaviour 64
Sports Aid 81
Sports Club 67
Sprains 48
Static Strength 25
Stimulants 56
Stitch 50
Strains 48
Stretching Exercises 29
Stroke Volume 13

Substance Abuse 56
Swimming 42
Synovial Joints 6, 7
Systolic Pressure 13

T

Technology 59
Temperature Regulation 37
Tendons 9
Testing Flexibility 29
Testing Speed 27
Tidal Volume 15
Tobacco 56
Torn Cartilage 49
Training 25, 35
Training Aids 59
Training Methods 31

U

UK Sport 75, 82, 83

V

VO_2 Max 15
Veins 11, 12
Vertebral Column 6
Videos 59
Vital Capacity 15
Vitamins 21
Voluntary Muscles 9

W

Warm Weather Training 34
Water 21, 22
Water Balance 37
Weight Training 31
White Cells 12
Working Energy 20

NOTES

Our Student Workbook matches this revision guide 'page for page' and provides great practice questions and excellent homework material.